Talking Heads
REMAIN IN LIGHT

Laura Shenton

Talking Heads
REMAIN IN LIGHT

Laura Shenton

WP
WYMER
PUBLISHING
Bedford, England

First published in 2022 by Wymer Publishing
Bedford, England www.wymerpublishing.co.uk Tel: 01234 326691
Wymer Publishing is a trading name of Wymer (UK) Ltd

Copyright © 2022 Laura Shenton / Wymer Publishing. This edition published 2022.

Print edition (fully illustrated): **ISBN: 978-1-912782-01-1**

Edited by Jerry Bloom.

The Author hereby asserts her rights to be identified
as the author of this work in accordance with sections
77 to 78 of the Copyright, Designs & Patents Act 1988.

All rights reserved. No part of this publication may be
reproduced or transmitted in any form or by any means,
electronic or mechanical, including photocopying, or any
information storage and retrieval system, without written
permission from the publisher.

This publication is sold subject to the condition that it shall not,
by way of trade or otherwise, be lent, re-sold, hired out or
otherwise circulated without the publishers' prior consent in any
form of binding or cover other than that in which it is published
and without a similar condition including this condition
being imposed on the subsequent purchaser.

eBook formatting by Coinlea.
Printed and bound in Great Britain by
CMP, Dorset.

A catalogue record for this book is available from the British Library.

Typeset by Andy Bishop / 1016 Sarpsborg
Cover design by 1016 Sarpsborg.
Cover photo © Gijsbert Hanekroot/ Alamy Stock Photo.

Contents

Preface   7

Chapter One: Why Remain In Light?   11

Chapter Two: The Making of Remain In Light   27

Chapter Three: The Tour   69

Chapter Four: Legacy   83

Discography   98

Tour Dates   105

"When I was in art school, somebody once said to me that the problem with you young artists is that you all want to be famous. When you get older you realise what's important to you — and Ralph Steadman, the cartoonist, said this — what becomes important to you is the charm of the activity. You live for the work, not for the money or for the fame. The success that is perhaps obvious to someone else is much less obvious to you."

- Tina Weymouth, 1980

"The good stuff for me is really pretty funky. It has trouble crossing over into the pop market. It's certainly better to dance to than a lot of other stuff. I just can't imagine dancing to rock 'n' roll. People do it — I seem to have forgotten how."

- David Byrne, 1981

Preface

'Once In A Lifetime' is one of those songs where, even if someone isn't a fan of Talking Heads, chances are they will have heard it. It's a fascinating song not only in terms of its uniqueness but in terms of how it so often divides opinion. Some would describe it as catchy and innovative whilst others may count it as being something that gets stuck in their head — even if they'd rather that it didn't!

This book will go some of the way towards investigating *how* and *why* 'Once In A Lifetime' has those opinion-dividing qualities about it. More than that though, the scope is much broader here. For of course, 'Once In A Lifetime', although the most well known, is one of eight tracks that make up Talking Heads' 1980 album, *Remain In Light*. Really, in terms of the artistic and technical musicianship and recording techniques embraced by Talking Heads — along with Brian Eno and other recruited talent — 'Once In A Lifetime' is just the tip of the iceberg.

As author of this book, my bias towards *Remain In Light* (and indeed Talking Heads overall) is inevitably a positive one. Despite this, I want to offer something factual rather than something that is peppered with my own opinion and interpretation of the music. You won't see any of that whole kind of "this section makes use of a 6/8 time signature and it therefore means X" or "I think this lyric means Y". For of course, the beauty of a lot of Talking Heads' music is in the ambiguity. It is not my place to throw a lot of my own opinions out there because it wouldn't add anything to the literature in doing so.

Talking Heads - *Remain In Light*: In-depth

The purpose of this book is to look at *Remain In Light* in detail: an extent of detail that has been put out there by those who worked on the album in terms of what their intentions were, and detail as in how the finished product was perceived at the time. As a result, throughout this book you're going to see lots of quotes from vintage articles. I think it's important to corroborate such material as there will probably come a time when it is harder to source.

In the interest of transparency, I have no affiliation with any of the artists involved in the making of *Remain In Light*, or with any of their associates. This book is based on extensive research and objective commentary.

Talking Heads - *Remain In Light*: In-depth

Chapter One

Why Remain In Light?

Remain In Light *is Talking Heads' fourth studio album. Released in October 1980 on Sire Records, it peaked at number nineteen on the US Billboard 200 and at number twenty-one in the UK. Spawning the singles 'Once In A Lifetime' and 'Houses In Motion', it has gone on to be featured in several publications' lists of the best albums of the 1980s (and, for that matter, of all time).

One of the most distinctive features of *Remain In Light* is in its experimental approach to sound. It was widely praised for it — both by critics and by the record-buying public. The fact that Talking Heads had succeeded to merge such an unlikely range of ideas together was applauded in abundance.

Remain In Light is a difficult album to categorise owing to the number of musical styles that it draws influence from. It has been categorised by music critics under a vast range of umbrellas: new wave, worldbeat, post-punk, art pop, dance rock, pop, avant-pop, funk, Afrofunk, Afrobeat. Even psychedelic and psychedelic funk. It's understandable considering that the eight tracks on the album make use of African rhythmic devices, funk bass, keyboards and electronics. Producer Brian Eno has said that the album uniquely blends funk, punk rock and new wave music.

Not only did the use of a wide range of musical influences add to the album's originality, but so did the way in which several musicians from a range of musical backgrounds were brought in to work on it.

Talking Heads - *Remain In Light*: In-depth

Excitingly, whilst *Remain In Light* was still in the works, *New Musical Express* reported in July 1980; "Eno's latest work is the as yet unreleased album with David Byrne, 'consciously affected by' the African music in which both have immersed themselves, though Eno insists that he can't say 'it's as good as that is'... Anyone who figures to have Eno already pigeonholed will get a shock when the contents are made public. The record moves to rhythm and patterns which are obviously not bland, overlaid with a thinking man's sense of melody, and much Eno-esque humour."

Up until 1979, Talking Heads were pretty much regarded as part of the new wave scene. Their music was occasionally even categorised as punk (such was the nature of the music press being keen to have explicit means of being able to categorise every up-and-coming band). Although Talking Heads were recognised as being a little quirky up to that point, like most other bands at the time, they would write the songs before getting to work in the studio. With *Remain In Light* though, that would change.

What makes *Remain In Light* a standout album is the fact that it draws upon so many influences that are often ignored in popular music (it was the case at the time and is still pretty much the case today). Talking Heads drew upon such influences as Fela Kuti and indeed, African music as a whole in its use of polyrhythms. With that, was the use of funk, electronic music, and indeed innovative musicianship for the purpose of looping and sequencing.

Critics gave *Remain In Light* widespread acclaim, with many of them regarding the album as a brave attempt to do something different. Not only that, but the album was largely regarded as an enjoyable instance of where usually opposing genres of music had been blended together so successfully. Overall, the album's innovative nature was welcomed rather than scorned. Impressive considering that with something so

Why Remain In Light?

unique, the response could have so easily been at the other end of the critical spectrum. Critical appreciation of the album was more than fleeting. In August 1981, *Melody Maker* referred to it as being "ground-breaking".

On balance, as a result of the success of their previous albums — *Talking Heads: 77*, *More Songs About Buildings And Food* and *Fear Of Music* — Talking Heads already had a loyal following of fans but it would seem flawed to assume that the success of *Remain In Light* was built on that basis alone.

Besides, some even considered that Talking Heads' new direction would be a disappointment to fans who had keenly supported the band's earlier output. New York's *Daily News* opined in October 1980; "The Manhattan underground's great commercial hope, Talking Heads, have made the most startling transition of all with the funky African tribal stomp of *Remain In Light* on their fourth album. For old-time Heads fans, the new direction may seem a bit of a letdown. But where the approach works, as on the startling psychedelic vision of 'Once In A Lifetime' or the angular Euro-disco raw funk fusion of 'Crosseyed And Painless', the results are impressive indeed."

From *The Tampa Tribune*: "New York's art-rock darlings have been exposed to African music, and this new collection is filled with polyrock rhythms and pulsating crosscurrents over chanting and multi-tracked vocals. With all this going on, we need an anchor, but the Heads leave the listener alone to cope or fall away. David Byrne's psychotic vocals remain low in the overall mix, lessening his threatening presence. The lyrics bear little resemblance to traditional song lyrics but are better communicated through the enclosed lyric sheet where eccentric typography aids understanding to this musical melange. There's nothing here as riveting as 'Take Me To The River', their cover of the Al Green song, or as obviously chilling as the songs on *Fear Of Music* or as easy as 'Psycho Killer'. This is a breakthrough conceptually for the Talking Heads. It remains to be seen whether their fans can break through with them."

Some critics at the time insisted that many rock and punk fans wouldn't be interested in funk and R&B. Talking Heads were in a good position to be able to deliver those styles commercially though, probably on the basis that their fanbase had already come to expect a sound that was quirky and at least somewhat against the grain.

It wasn't that *Remain In Light* took Talking Heads from an absolute lack of success to the other end of the spectrum but overall, the album served to mark the fact that in the grand scheme of things, they had come a long way. One journalist considered in early 1981; "Who can blame David Byrne if he sounds a little surprised by his current success? Six years ago he was a reject from the Rhode Island School of Design, living in a slum on the Lower East Side and working as a movie usher. Today many critics are calling him the foremost composer in rock music, the man most instrumental in creating new wave."

Considering the breadth and depth of new wave, although the last sentence there could be argued as being something of an overstatement, the fact is that with *Remain In Light* to his credit, there was no denying Byrne's — and indeed the rest of Talking Heads' — success.

So how were Talking Heads regarded when their album prior to *Remain In Light*, *Fear Of Music*, was at the forefront of their reputation? *New Musical Express* considered in December 1979; "Okay, so *Fear Of Music* didn't go mega platinum in the first month of its release. Okay, so the brilliant single, 'Life During Wartime', failed to secure a prestigious chart placing in either the British or the US top twenties. But make no mistake, 1979 has been Talking Heads' most lucrative year to date. The album's disquieting tonal quality, bizarre conceits and uneasy listening somehow still managed to grant it a cosy location in the lower reaches of the American top thirty whilst affording it across-the-board rave reviews. Indeed, when we

Why Remain In Light?

here at the NME sweatshop were called upon to scribble down our favourite albums of the year, *Fear Of Music* shut down its nearest rival by almost two votes to one. *Fear Of Music* is in fact a grand departure from the previous two Talking Heads albums, *77* and *More Songs About Buildings And Food*. The latter pair, although different in a number of key respects that arguably have the most to do with a change of producer — Tony Bongiovi handled *77* whilst *Buildings* saw the commencement of a most fruitful alliance with Brian Eno — are tied together by one key factor in that, as Byrne himself only too readily admits, 'The first two albums featured and consequently used up all the songs I'd written within a certain space of time. I had absolutely nothing left in reserve for *Fear Of Music* and therefore had to get to grips with composing a whole new set of songs.' Listening to the three records certainly bears this point out."

"On *77* Byrne's melodies are more expansive, with songs like 'The Book I Read', 'Pulled Up' and 'Happy Day' bristling with strong hook-lines, whilst the Frantz/Weymouth rhythm section, having not yet fully developed into the earth-shudderingly functional power they now are, were still getting over the restriction of having once been two-thirds of a three-piece band and were content to work on their personalised retreading of the base-and-drums interplay notable on the Al Green records they used to practice from ceaselessly. These factors, along with producer Bongiovi's inability to capture a band as a fully interlocking four-piece (although Jerry Harrison's extra textures on keyboards and second guitar had already been tightly meshed into the band's live sound, his contributions were virtually ignored on the first album), provided the inquisitive listener with a debut album spotlighting Byrne's quirky song structures and lyrics. Mated to a pleasantly buoyant rhythm section, it made for a marketable coalition of left-field disco and agreeable new wave: an utterly superficial conclusion, of course, but in an industry where labels seem all-important, an equation needed to be formulated. The stand-out track on *77* was 'Psycho Killer' which, although Byrne shrugs off the contention that the song has since become a proverbial albatross around the group's neck, has certainly granted many reviewers the perfect vehicle for nailing Talking Heads to the psyco-rock mast head."

Byrne elaborated; "'Psycho Killer' was the first song I ever wrote. Alice Cooper was really big then and I just thought it'd be interesting to do a song in something approaching that mock-ghoulish vein he was pumping, but give certain twists. Alice Cooper had all these safety gauges worked out so that it wouldn't connect with anything remotely dangerous. It was all 'It's okay folks, it's only a show'. I just liked the idea of writing a song that was more *real*."

With a new decade on the horizon, the variety of musical genres that graced the charts in the late seventies was a fascinating mixture. There was punk, disco, and rock — to name a few! After all, 1979 saw the following albums do well in both the UK and the US: Pink Floyd's *The Wall*, Michael Jackson's *Off The Wall*, and Blondie's *Parallel Lines*. In terms of genre, it could be said that by 1980, commercial success was there to be had by just about anybody who dared to have a shot at it.

Around this time, although Talking Heads were often abundantly labelled as a new wave band, they were predominantly part of New York's punk scene. That was largely riding on the coattails of the rejection of the more established rock music of the seventies. Whilst punk, to many, was embedded in the idea that music should be about spontaneously and rebelliously performing anger and angst, in comparison, Talking Heads were very much a different animal. Whilst other punk bands shouted lyrics about the establishment, Byrne's lyrics centred more on everyday subjects (for instance, 'The Book I Read' on *77* and

Why Remain In Light?

'Found A Job' on *Buildings*). Added to that, his vocal style was unusual and the way he moved on stage was in a league of its own — close to awkwardness but never fully uncomfortable. Essentially, his dancing was almost ironic. Compared to what other groups were doing — even where their music could be just slightly linked — Talking Heads were strange. But strange enough to be interesting. Of the band's name, Byrne explained, "We got the name from TV. A "talking heads" show is one where people talk in a studio, like *Meet The Press*."

It would be flawed to say that Talking Heads had nothing in common with the punk scene though. In terms of how the band were from an art school background rather than a traditional music one, Byrne told *New Musical Express* in December 1981; "None of us were skilled musicians. We hadn't played around for ten years and then all of a sudden had a hit. I think that's true for a lot of bands."

Commenting on the music media at the time, Brian Eno told *New Musical Express* in July 1980; "All the papers have got involved in a fairly local ideological struggle. They've all taken new wave and punk much more seriously than any new musicians I know. For the musicians it was not even a defined form as such. No one who was working in that area saw such clear boundaries and definitions and meaning as writers have. And it seems to me now that they have made such a heavy emotional investment that they have to put a lot of distance between themselves and anything which does not fit into a certain area."

At a time when most other punk artists prided their act on being authentic and musically stripped down to basics, Talking Heads were more willing to experiment. The Byrne-led band first performed under the Talking Heads name in 1975 when they opened for the Ramones at CBGB. Back then, Talking Heads was a trio consisting of Byrne on vocals and guitar, Tina Weymouth on bass, and Chris Frantz on drums. It wasn't until just before the release of their first studio album, *Talking Heads: 77*, that keyboardist and guitarist Jerry Harrison joined.

The quartet started their collaboration with Brian Eno as producer when they made *More Songs About Buildings And Food* in 1978. Such collaboration continued for their 1979 album, *Fear Of Music*.

Even in their early days, Talking Heads were not afraid to experiment: to go with the flow and see where the music would take them. "There is something essential about losing control over what you do," said Weymouth in 1977. And to think that without such determination, the band could have evolved into something different entirely!

New Musical Express commented in November 1980; "*Remain In Light* is, as others have pointed out, a transitional album. Talking Heads keep making transitional albums. But they follow a certain path. It's hard to believe that four years ago they willingly let producer Matthew King Kaufman try to turn them into the perfect bubblegum band on a set of demos that have since been lost."

Within this, it's clear that Talking Heads felt no obligation to follow a perhaps, more commercially reliable path. Byrne told *New Musical Express* in December 1981; "I'm not sure what kind of tradition we belong to. We've sort of stuck ourselves in pop music and we're in that business and yet we and a lot of other bands in the last five years or so, I'm sure none of us really feel like we're continuing a tradition of that music. We probably all feel like we snuck in here, snuck into the business and we haven't been found out yet... I think traditional rock 'n' roll is one sort of romanticism that is *valid*, but it's not one that I find particularly interesting or that I think I'm very good at. I think there's a lot of other possibilities, so I guess I sort of ignore that one a little bit."

And of course, from a commercial point of view, Afrobeat is a different field entirely. It owes much of its distinctive

Why Remain In Light?

qualities to the scope it gives musicians to be spontaneous. So, what is Afrobeat? Well, it combines elements of West African musical styles such as fújì and highlife with American jazz and later soul and funk influences. Afrobeat places emphasis on chanted vocals and complex use of weaving rhythms (often contributed via percussion). Fela Kuti coined the term in the mid-sixties and it was he who predominantly popularised the style both in and beyond Nigeria (his birthplace).

The term polyrhythm is often mentioned under the umbrella of Afrobeat. A polyrhythm is the simultaneous use of two or more rhythms that are not readily perceived as deriving from one another, or as simple manifestations of the same meter. For a polyrhythm to be present, at least two rhythms need to be played together — either as the basis for an entire piece of music or as a small part thereof. In basic terms, a polyrhythm is when the music features multiple layers of rhythms. Whilst the technical structure of Western classical music was built on complexities of harmonies and tone, the traditional music of West Africa was built on a foundation of complex interweaving of contrasting rhythmic patterns. So much so that it is a vital aspect of what gives African music its distinctive charisma.

A good example of how a polyrhythm superimposes beats in different time signatures over one another can be heard in isolation in the opening bars of Kuti's 'Why Black Man Dey Suffer'. In this example, three sets of triplets cut over the (relatively loose!) time signature before they go on to build up into to a complete rhythm. Technical complexities aside, essentially, Afrobeat is designed with movement in mind: it exists to fire the listener up via an infectiously catchy bout of rhythm.

Afrobeat's popularity rose in Ghana and Nigeria during the seventies. Fela Kuti was a key pioneer of this. Eno actually played Kuti's 1973 *Afrodisiac* album to Byrne the night that they met in 1977.

Talking Heads - *Remain In Light*: In-depth

Eno told *New Musical Express* in July 1980; "Maybe I can make the people of England forsake their new wave records and rush out to buy Fela Kuti! Actually, I just hope people listen to it. He's one of the leading exponents of high life music, but there are plenty of others. It's a beautiful music — it's so thrilling to me. I could work twenty-four hours a day on this music. It's rhythmically sophisticated in an interesting way; it's perfect for dancing because it leaves holes in all the right places — it pulls your body in a most interesting way. Like the great revolution of reggae was that it left a hole somewhere where rock music always puts it in. And that poises your body on a precipice so you're constantly kept in motion. You listen to this and you can't help but think 'What do *we* have? The fucking Jam!' I've had this record since '72 or '73, but lately I've been listening to high life and African pop music quite a lot."

Talking Heads had already explored polyrhythms on *Fear Of Music* on the track 'I Zimbra', of which Byrne told *Melody Maker* in August 1981; "It was sort of a first stab at that kind of thing. Then as we went on I got a little more involved in that. I still am." On *Remain In Light*, the opening track of 'Born Under Punches (The Heat Goes On)' gets to it in very much the same way. Multilayered guitar, bass, and drum patterns are technically complex but simply, catchy and demanding of attention.

The use of rhythm on *Remain In Light* is phenomenal. It often adds more weight to the words, such as in the case of 'Crosseyed And Painless'. An idea that starts out as being downright catchy, goes on to provide an intensity that stays with the listener.

Although *Remain In Light* is now largely recognised as a classic album, there is so much about it that still sounds fresh. It breaks away from the more conventional, expected forms typically used in rock and pop music. On 'Crosseyed And Painless' for instance, Weymouth's bassline is abundant

Why Remain In Light?

in staccato notes in the first half of a measure and then there is nothing on that front for the second half. The result is a percussive pattern that is more commonly present in funk and essentially, it is attention-grabbing on the basis that it is not what most consumers of pop music would expect to hear.

Harrison uses his guitar as a source of atmospheric noise rather than as a means through which to play riffs. On 'Listening Wind' it creates an eerie feeling of atmosphere.

In the grand scheme of things, Talking Heads had always been a multidimensional band. It seemed to come naturally to them. Byrne told *New Musical Express* in December 1981; "I think it's much easier if a band or a singer or whatever has one identity; they seem to have one character or one personality. If they start displaying too many facets of their character, it can be confusing. I think I tend to do that. Can't help it, I guess. I think it's realistic. People do have lots of facets to their character, they're not just one-dimensional things."

Melody Maker considered in August 1981; "It's ironic that the Heads should have achieved their greatest commercial success after moving away from the more straightforward pop/rock structure which permeated their first couple of albums, though *Fear Of Music* saw the beginnings of the new approach, especially in 'I Zimbra'."

New Musical Express observed in July 1979; "'I Zimbra', utilises an African rhythm, lush percussive effects treated by some spectacular synthesiser colouration. It's the kind of deceptively simple sound that Brian Eno experimented with on *Taking Tiger Mountain (By Strategy)* or 'The Lion Sleeps Tonight', but with a more integrated, less self-conscious appeal. The vocal is a multi-layered nonsense babble, African Esperanto. Towards the end, Robert Fripp contributes a fragment of a solo. Byrne has a selection of South African music with him, notably *Rhythm Of Resistance*."

Really, it could be argued that the genius of *Remain In*

Talking Heads - *Remain In Light*: In-depth

Light (yep, genius) is that although it goes against so much of what is expected from a commercially successful album, it does it so well that it speaks to a wide range of listeners with a just-as-wide preference towards genres. *Remain In Light* is in a league of its own.

Remain In Light invites the listener not only to engage with and enjoy the music, but to think. Why? Simply because it is so substantially different to any other album — in terms of the mixture of influences it makes use of and in terms of what the result actually is.

Why Remain In Light?

Talking Heads - *Remain In Light*: In-depth

Aesthetic elitism meets expediency

(NB: This is an intelligent review)

TALKING HEADS
'Remain In Light'
(Sire SRK 6095)***

WELL ALRIGHT, I may never be going back to my old school, but I remember a saying they had out in the yard that's one of the few things I picked up there to continue to be of use through the years. It went: *"Tell us news, not history"*.

At a time when Waits, Cooder and Springsteen are proving the existence of valid life in the old dog of traditionalist rock 'n' roll,

Archive Tapes Menace, Young Ones EP

Talking Heads are the only members of the consciously innovatory mob residing at the end of the waveband who manage to intrigue *and* chart without descending to the simplistic compositional slumming of the Numanoids.

While scanning that fast tour of modern art *The Shock Of The New* on the old cathode tube the other night, I was struck by the narrator's comments on some pieces of furniture designed by a passionate bright young thing earlier this century; a sleek, streamlined chair looked clever-clever for sure, but 'unfortunately it just wasn't any good for sitting in. I immediately thought of rock, always behind other art forms by some years, which is only now reaching the point where it's producing groups that appear smart but are *utterly useless*. Talking Heads, being streets ahead of most of the art/rock pack, aren't like that at all; they combine aesthetisicm with real-life practicality, they get Brian Eno to produce an album that'll serve those who want a George Clinton record without the Process church guff.

'Remain In Light' is, like Talking Heads albums, an extension of their past and something new, too. Side consists of 3 lengthy funk episodes. 'Born Under Punches (The Heat Goes O is percussive and fingerpopping, as in Parliament if they'd had th coke'n'limo rug pulled swi from under them, while Da Byrne sings, as ever, with the alienation of the Eleph Man. The concerns are familiar: *"government ma "take a look at these hands "I'm too thin"*.

The body-rhythms conti in 'Cross Eyed And Painles which doesn't sound like a single but does echo arour combination sandwich of ' During Wartime' and 'Air', while Byrne talks of *"wasting away"*. The fina strut is 'The Great Curve', which is not about Jayne Mansfield but is about a sophisticated mix and som stunning guitar which sour sure to be coming from Ac Belew, Bowie's latest axeman, who's credited as playing on this album with reference to any particular cut, as are Robert Palmer (percussion) and Nona

Why Remain In Light?

TALKING HEADS, phunk without phoney phlash

...dryx (throat). The flip's five songs lead with 'Once In A Lifetime', ...ile Jerry Harrison, and ...tion folks Tina ...ymouth/Chris Frantz ...thm it away more Detroit ...n ever, Byrne speaks his ...s about an index of ...sible life situations in a ...ce that's a cross 'tween ...ody Allen and a TV real ...ate commercial, before an ...e chorus vocal explodes ...h a *trés* African melody, ...f the words buzz about *...ater flowing underground''* ...ets the appetite for .../Byrne's upcoming Afro-chedelic elpee, and could well be a hit 45 your mum would hum.

'Houses In Motion', on the other hand, is very *film-noir*, with a typically ethno-Amazonian trumpet and horn arrangement by Eno-pal Jon Hassel, while 'Seen And Not Seen' is a funk-narrative involving bizarre physical metamorphosis for the central character, and 'The Listening Wind' seems to evoke eastern terrorism, hypnotically portraying the protagonist as devout boy rapt in mysticism and faith. An interesting counterpoint to the way the theme of organised urban violence was pictured in 'Life During Wartime' on 'Fear Of Music', the Head's last LP. The grabby aural treacle of the final cut, 'The Overload', might be about breakdown, or even meltdown. Might be. It *might* as well be 'The Overlook'.

No-one else in the rock strata does these things. You have to look to jazz, and then to the work of Arthur Blythe specifically (whose discs I commend to you), to find someone using traditions in new ways, *thinking* about the present with a *feeling* for the past. Talking Heads are telling us news. Not history.

SANDY ROBERTSON

Talking Heads - *Remain In Light*: In-depth

Chapter Two

The Making of Remain In Light

After the release of Talking Heads' third album — *Fear Of Music* — in August 1979, along with Brian Eno, the band were keen to dispel the notion that Talking Heads was merely a vehicle through which to serve David Byrne as a frontman. Following their tour in support of the album, Talking Heads were back in New York by January 1980. Their first priority was to pursue projects away from the band. David Byrne worked with Brian Eno on the experimental album, *My Life In The Bush Of Ghosts*.

Already a married couple by this point, Chris Frantz and Tina Weymouth were already considering leaving Talking Heads on the basis that Weymouth considered Byrne to be too controlling. With Frantz not wanting to leave the band though, the two took a long vacation to the Caribbean to think things over. It was there that they got involved in Haitian Vodou religious ceremonies, played native percussion instruments, and socialised with the Jamaican rhythm duo, Sly and Robbie (drummer Sly Dunbar and bassist Robbie Shakespeare).

Towards the end of their holiday, Frantz and Weymouth purchased an apartment above Compass Point Studios in Nassau, the Bahamas. Talking Heads had recorded their second album there — *More Songs About Buildings And Food*. In early 1980, all four members of Talking Heads met up there and upon this, everyone agreed that even though the band was a quartet, everything had been left up to Byrne when it came to crafting the songs. It was also agreed that the format of lead singer plus backing band was one that wasn't the format that anybody had in mind for Talking Heads anymore. As a result, as Byrne put it, everyone decided that it was time for "sacrificing our egos for mutual cooperation". On top of this, Byrne wanted to get away from what he referred to as "the psychological paranoia and personal torment" that he had been feeling — and consequently writing — in New York.

For the album that would become *Remain In Light*, the modus operandi was that instead of the band writing something to fit with Byrne's lyrics, the songs would be born out of instrumental jams. In such regard, 'I Zimbra' from *Fear Of Music* was referred to as a starting point.

When asked to explain his general approach to songwriting, Byrne told *New Musical Express* in December 1981; "Most of the time the words come last, although they may not be written last, they may be written simultaneously but separately — I just collect a lot of lyrics. I think usually I'll start with a rhythm or a texture in mind; sometimes a rhythm is a way of achieving a kind of texture — a lot of times I'll go after that instead of going after a specific melody. Which, to me, that's what music's been about in the last thirty years or so and it's more about that now than it ever was before. More about rhythm and texture and less about the topline melody. Songs in the past before records and sophisticated recording were so common, you wouldn't be surprised to see someone trying to play 'She's A Bad Mamajama' or something on the piano. It just seems that songs aren't about that anymore."

Eno turned up in the Bahamas three weeks after Talking Heads had all been there together. He was actually reluctant to work with the band again having already collaborated with them on their last two albums. It was upon being played the demo tapes for the new project that he changed his mind.

With Eno, Talking Heads started to experiment with the idea of how individual rhythms can be meshed together into

The Making of Remain In Light

polyrhythms. Fela Kuti's 1973 album, *Afrodisiac*, played a strong influence in this. Additionally, as Weymouth went on to explain, Talking Heads was highly aware of how the landscape of popular music was changing what with how early hip-hop music was a big part of the New York scene. That's not to say that the approach to *Remain In Light* was prescriptive though.

As the band's friend David Gans put it to them before the studio sessions for the album had even started: "The things one doesn't intend are the seeds for a more interesting future." As part of this, he encouraged them to be experimental in improvising and to make use of material that would usually be all too readily dismissed as "mistakes".

In terms of wishing to point out the futility of striving for intensively meaningful lyrics, Gans also opined to Byrne that "rational thinking has its limits".

Over the July and August of 1980, *Remain In Light* was recorded at Compass Point Studios in the Bahamas as well as at Sigma Sound Studios in Philadelphia. It would be the last of Talking Heads' albums to be produced by Brian Eno.

In July 1980 at Compass Point Studios, the recording sessions began. Sections and instrumentals were recorded one at a time in a discontinuous process. Looping what had been recorded was a key aspect of making the album — and all before computers were adequately able to perform such function. Talking Heads recorded jam sessions and then isolated the best parts. They would then learn to play them repetitively. Essentially, the looping was done by the musicians themselves rather than by employing the use of technology to do it for them. Byrne said in later years, "We were human samplers."

From having worked with Eno on *My Life In The Bush Of Ghosts* prior to *Remain In Light*, Byrne had confidence that "a pop record could indeed be made in that way."

Even outside of his work with Talking Heads, Eno had a firm interest in how the recording studio could be used to maximise the scope for creativity. He had recently given some lectures on the subject in San Francisco and at the University of California, Berkeley when in July 1980 he told *New Musical Express* what they had been about; "The recording studio as a compositional tool: there were two strands in the talk. One was talking about the special compositional possibilities that the recording studio offers as distinct from any other compositional mode. The other strand was actually saying that this is actually a new form of art. I want to talk at an interesting level about how technical possibilities give rise to conceptual possibilities and vice-versa. For instance, how the possibility that you could completely reorganise the dynamic structure of a piece of music gave rise to funk. The fact that you could have a bass and a bass drum extremely loud in a way that wasn't possible in an ordinary playing environment can give rise to a whole form of music anchored round those two things, around the rhythm section."

"The lecture was in three parts. The first was history, technical history. The second was subsequent possibilities, and the third part was talking about my own use of the medium and my feelings about what kind of future that offered and also the interesting artistic question of 'why this now?'. That's always the question critics should be answering and they hardly ever do. Why should this form evolve now rather than then? It's not only technical possibilities: there are clearly strong cultural reasons why things appear at a time. Not only why they suddenly appear, but why everyone suddenly likes them. Look at the ska revolution. I can remember listening to Prince Buster in 1964. It's been there for ages and ages. Then there's a shift in public consciousness which makes it the form people want to hear."

"I've always assumed that culture is a unity," he continued. "I assume that cultural events don't happen in isolation from one another and that if a whole series of things are happening at one time, it's interesting to try and make a complete picture of them and to try and include everything in that picture. For instance, my cultural picture of England at the moment says ska — a return of a particular style of clothing which is a low fashion rather than a high fashion sensibility — Conservative government — disenchantment with labour structures. Any created picture should try to accommodate all those facts rather than just pop music or what gets called rock culture. Things happen for one of two reasons: either because people want them or because they don't want the alternative. Governments obviously often happen for the latter reason; wherever the choice is simple and binary you get a lot of that negative thing. The other factor is time lags; certain things like fashion are very rapidly-changing forms."

Every track on *Remain In Light* was built up by the band focussing on rhythms — so much so that they were all performed in a minimalist fashion using only one chord. None of the songs on *Remain In Light* include chord changes. Instead, they rely on the use of different harmonics and notes. Every section was recorded as a long loop. This enabled the creation of compositions whereby loops could then be merged and positioned in different ways.

For every song on *Remain In Light*, the rhythm was the first thing to be laid down: sometimes drums alone, and other times drums and bass together.

Following the small number of sessions in the Bahamas, engineer Rhett Davies had abandoned the project after an argument over the speed at which the recording was being done. His role was taken over by Steven Stanley. Frantz said that Stanley was key in the creation of 'Once In A Lifetime'.

Engineer and mixer Dave Jerden obtained a Lexicon 224 digital reverb effects unit. Used on the album, the machine was one of the first of its kind able to simulate environments such as echo chambers and rooms through interchangeable programs. Like Davies, Jerden wasn't happy about the fast pace at which

Talking Heads - *Remain In Light*: In-depth

Eno wanted to record such sonically complicated compositions. It was not to the extent that it was a point of confrontation though.

It was during the making of *Remain In Light* that Byrne started to rethink his vocal style. Few vocal sections were recorded in the Bahamas and it was when the band returned to the US and was split between New York City and California that the writing of the lyrics happened. Harrison booked Talking Heads into Sigma Sound. The studio had a reputation for focusing predominantly on R&B music. Harrison had to convince the owners of the studio that letting Talking Heads work there could encourage a new range of clientele to make bookings.

Whilst in New York City, Byrne struggled with writer's block. Whilst Harrison and Eno spent their time tweaking the compositions that had been recorded in the Bahamas, Frantz and Weymouth would often not show up at the studio. The issues were such that doubts began to surface regarding whether the album could be completed. It was via the recruitment of former Frank Zappa/David Bowie guitarist Adrian Belew that the recording sessions picked up in vital momentum. Byrne, Harrison and Eno were all instrumental in the recruitment of Belew. He was advised to add guitar solos to the tracks recorded at Compass Point that had made use of a Roland guitar synthesiser.

It was after Belew's contribution to all of the tracks that Byrne started to work on them. Looking to African music for inspiration, he took note of how when African musicians forget words, they often improvise and make new ones up. Using a portable tape recorder, he tried to create onomatopoeic rhymes in the style of Eno, who would often advocate that lyrics should never be at the centre of a song's meaning.

Byrne continuously listened to his recorded scatting until convinced that he was no longer "hearing nonsense". From there, Harrison invited Nona Hendryx to Sigma Sound to contribute backing vocals to the album. Byrne, Frantz and Weymouth gave detailed directions on what they expected from her vocal delivery. The vocal sessions — on which Byrne and Eno contributed — were followed by the overdubbing process.

Brass player Jon Hassell, who had already worked with Eno on *Fourth World, Vol. 1: Possible Musics*, was hired to perform trumpet and horn sections. In August 1980, half of the album was mixed by Eno and engineer John Potoker in New York City with the assistance of Harrison, whilst the other half was mixed by Byrne and Jerden at Eldorado Studios in Los Angeles.

The Songs

Byrne and Eno share credit for the lyrics on 'Born Under Punches (The Heat Goes On)'. The song is about life in a paranoid version of America (post-Watergate scandal). It centres on the struggle of an ordinary working-class man who is taking a metaphorical pummelling from the government. With a lyric like "all I want is to breathe," there is a sense of a cry for help that comes across. Byrne sings of being a tumbler. With the latter being an acrobatic clown responsible for doing rolls and flips, the lyrics allude to the idea of someone who has no choice but to roll with the punches — no matter what the system throws at them. *Melody Maker* considered in August 1981; "Byrne takes infinite pains in his disassociations. Consider the dialogue between singer and chorus in 'Born Under Punches', where questions are sometimes posed and answered, sometimes deflected and diffused."

'Born Under Punches' features a steady rhythm that continues without change. With no variation in this regard, it could be said that the song relies more on the lyrics. Another instance of where the vocal lines contribute to this is where

Talking Heads - *Remain In Light*: In-depth

Brian Eno quotes a headline from the *New York Post* about a heat wave.

A friend of Talking Heads and working nearby to them at the time, Robert Palmer played on a small Brazilian drum. This contribution was used for the overdub on 'Born Under Punches'.

A journalist interviewing Byrne for *Melody Maker* in August 1981 reported; "Borrowings can come from anywhere. The fast guitar strum from Leon Haywood's 'Don't Push It Don't Force It' for instance, provided him with some impetus for 'Born Under Punches'."

The drum beat that features on 'Crosseyed And Painless' was inspired by the James Brown song, 'There Was A Time'.

Adrian Belew's guitar work on 'Crosseyed And Painless' is fast and strong. It certainly softened the blow of Eno being unable to get Robert Fripp to play on the album. In later years, Belew said of working on *Remain In Light*; "It seems to me like every time I tried to get a note to do a certain thing it just worked. I looked in the studio control room through the glass and I saw Jerry, David and Brian all kind of jumping up and down."

The "rhythmical rant" in 'Crosseyed And Painless' — 'Facts are simple and facts are straight. Facts are lazy and facts are late.' — was inspired by (what is now referred to as old school) rap; specifically, Kurtis Blow's 'The Breaks'.

Videos were made for 'Crosseyed And Painless' and 'Once In A Lifetime', both of which were directed by Toni Basil (yep, the Toni Basil famous for the 1982 hit single, 'Mickey'). Byrne had met Basil when in the early stages of working on *My Life In The Bush Of Ghosts*.

The video for 'Crosseyed And Painless' features street dancers who body pop their way through a number of scenarios, including a knife fight and other street hustles. Apparently, Talking Heads made a firm decision not to make an appearance

The Making of Remain In Light

in the video.

'Crosseyed And Painless' would go on to be played for the climax of Talking Heads' *Speaking In Tongues* era performances. An excellent choice of number to leave the audience energised and wanting more. The interlocking rhythms and scope for solos on 'Crosseyed And Painless' made it a strong choice to perform on stage.

The writing of 'The Great Curve' was born out of a jam session where Talking Heads improvised around a riff from the Fela Kuti song, 'Shuffering And Shmiling'. Byrne's idea was for the riff to start the song and then once the other instruments were added, the riff could be removed to leave behind an original song.

In creating the lyrics for 'The Great Curve', Byrne had been reading about the Yoruba people (who are mostly based in Nigeria). The Yoruba people have a concept of a maternal figurehead, a great woman or a great mother. The song is abundant in the African influence where it features the line 'The world moves on a woman's hips'. Byrne used it after he'd read Professor Robert Farris Thompson's book, *African Art In Motion*.

To finish off the track, Eno brought in Adrian Belew to lay down some solos in the gaps — a sensible idea given that there are no bridges and no middle eight in the song. Belew used a mute pedal to stop the long screaming notes dead in their tracks, a trick that he'd learned when recording with Eno and David Bowie on the *Lodger* album released in 1979.

Years later, Chris Frantz spoke of how 'The Great Curve' was a thrilling song to perform.

'Once In A Lifetime' started out as a jam that came to be labelled as 'Weird Guitar Riff Song'. Eno suggested that the band should build up from a foundation of just one or two chords where overdubs could be added later. It was from this basic foundation that Talking Heads came up with a firm idea that they named 'Right Start'. It was released as a bonus track on the 2006 reissue of *Remain In Light*, offering an insight into what the early version of 'Once In A Lifetime' sounded like. Eno wasn't happy with 'Right Start' — so much so that if he'd had his way, the idea would have been abandoned entirely.

'Once In A Lifetime' is almost trancelike. This is aided by the fact that it maintains the same pulsing rhythm all the way through. Interestingly, the drumbeat makes minimal use of cymbals. According to Harrison, "Because there were so few chord changes, and everything was in a sort of trance... it became harder to write defined choruses."

Weymouth recalled in later years how Frantz was calling across the studio at her what he thought the bassline needed to be. Upon taking his advice, that was the one. For his keyboard solo at the end of 'Once In A Lifetime', Harrison took inspiration from The Velvet Underground's song, 'What Goes On'.

Although 'Once In A Lifetime' pays homage to early rap techniques, Talking Heads made it very much their own. Regarding the use of almost-spoken voice (such as the preacher-inspired one on 'Once In A Lifetime'), Byrne told *New Musical Express* in December 1981; "It makes a comment in a literal way; the fact that their voices are impassioned means that it works very well with the music that has some sort of energy to it. If you just took a straight narrative — somebody telling a story or something — and stuck it on top of an energetic or rhythmic piece of music it'd seem out of place in a way." In December 1979, he told *New Musical Express* of the vocal lessons he'd attempted; "They weren't very successful. The coach kept wanting me to sing 'Send In The Clowns' and somehow I didn't see how."

And of course, the way in which Byrne took on a character in delivery of his vocals for 'Once In A Lifetime' certainly adds another layer of interest to the song. He told *New Musical Express* in December 1981; "You imagine the singer believes what they're saying, and it then helps you imagine yourself in that person's position. If songs were all sung in the third person it'd be a difficult task. It would make everybody seem like they were describing something that was very much outside of them."

Byrne said the song was a result of the band trying and failing to play funk, inadvertently creating something new instead.

The iconic riff was conceived as a single one before the band added a second, boosted riff on top of it. Eno alternated eight bars of each riff with corresponding bars of its counterpart.

Eno didn't like the baseline that Talking Heads were happy with. He went so far as to remove Weymouth's playing of it from the mix and then proceeded to add a different version himself. Upon hearing of this, Weymouth put her bassline back into the track after Eno was no longer working on it. Although the latter could be regarded as an indication that there were tensions between Eno and Weymouth, it's seemingly more plausible that this was just as a result of several creatives working together amongst a storm of interesting — and sometimes conflicting — ideas. Weymouth said in later years; "It wasn't a big fight between me and Brian, as it has sometimes been portrayed. It was just a musical dispute."

Eno's rhythmic interpretation of the riff was different to that of the other band members; he interpreted the third beat of the bar as the first. He urged the others to interpret the beat in different ways, thus providing the scope for different rhythmic elements to be exaggerated. He considered; "This means the song has a funny balance, with two centres of gravity — their funk groove, and my dubby, reggae-ish understanding of it; a bit like the way Fela Kuti songs will have multiple rhythms going on at the same time, warping in and out of each other."

After the basic track had been laid down and with placeholder vocals on tape, Byrne went away to work on the lyrics. It was around this time that he was studying the vocal delivery used by angelical preachers. He said in later years of how he applied that to writing the lyrics for 'Once In A Lifetime': "I kind of got myself up into this thing where I just started improvising this rant and I'd write it down and then structured it so that it fit the song. I thought it was like a preacher talking; I was imitating a preacher or it was a person kind of preaching to themselves about how alienated they felt. The chorus is the release — the person transcends that."

The song is about how one can sleepwalk through life when blindly committed to striving for social status symbols (such as the large automobile, the beautiful house and/or the beautiful wife).

It could be considered prophetic that 'Once In A Lifetime' was written at the beginning of a decade that would be remembered for attitudes of peak consumerism and greed. Importantly though, in later years, Byrne denied that the lyrics address yuppie greed, insisting that they are about the unconscious: "We operate half-awake or on autopilot and end up, whatever, with a house and family and job and everything else, and we haven't really stopped to ask ourselves, 'How did I get here?'"

Eno did an improvisation on the baptism motif from 'Take Me To The River'. He made it his own and it ended up being used for the chorus of 'Once In A Lifetime'.

The water theme mentioned in the chorus is also referenced in John Miller Chernoff's *African Rhythm And African Sensibility: Aesthetics And Social Action In African Musical Idioms*. It is also apparent in the 1975 Fela Kuti song, 'Water No Get Enemy'.

Professor John Miller Chernoff's text examined the musical enhancement of life in Africa's rural communities. The academic had travelled to Ghana in order to study native percussion. He subsequently wrote about how Africans have

The Making of Remain In Light

complicated conversations through drum patterns.

Eno told *New Musical Express* in July 1980; "There's a very good book I've been reading — *African Rhythm And African Sensibility* by John Miller Chernoff. David Byrne and I started getting into African music and culture — well, all the Talking Heads did — but David and I started work together which was very consciously influenced by it."

When promoting *Remain In Light*, Byrne and Eno gave the journalists due to carry out the interviews some reading materials (including but not limited to: John Miller Chernoff's piece, *African Art In Motion* by Robert Farris Thompson and *The Timeless Way Of Building* by Christopher Alexander). It was done in the hopes that it would inspire the journalists to formulate meaningful questions about the album.

Released as a single, 'Once In A Lifetime' got to number fourteen in the UK, to number twenty-three in Australia and to number twenty-eight in Canada. It flopped in the US though! That's not to say that it was ignored by the music press there. *Cash Box* reviewed it in January 1981; "If George Martin was, indeed, the "fifth Beatle", then Brian Eno deserves the honour of being named the "fifth Head", as his influence on the group's music is nowhere more apparent than on this rhythmically elliptical cut from the *Remain In Light* LP."

For the video, Byrne wore glasses, a bowtie and an oversized black suit. Behind him plays footage of religious rituals as well as a computerised model of water. As the only member of Talking Heads to appear in the video, Byrne preaches directly to the camera.

Byrne told *New Musical Express* in December 1981 that the character in the ill-fitting suit in the 'Once In A Lifetime' video "was meant to be a rural preacher. I had looked at a lot of films and read a bit about rural preachers and speaking in tongues and that sort of thing — the general phenomenon of religious ecstasy. So a lot of the movements were taken from that — I just thought, take some of these movements and abstract them, choreograph them, make it into a sort of spastic dance."

He had studied not only videos of religious rituals from the UCLA library, but Basil had shown him videos of people having epileptic fits. Both such materials informed Byrne's style of dancing in the 'Once In A Lifetime' video. According to Basil: "David kind of choreographed himself. I set up the camera, put him in front of it, and asked him to absorb those ideas. Then I left the room so he could be alone with himself. I came back, looked at the videotape, and we chose physical moves that worked with the music. I just helped to stylise his moves a little."

In order to put emphasis on Byrne's jerky movements, Basil used a zoom lens (she later described it as "old fashioned"). Indeed, the whole video was made on a low budget. Basil described it as "about as low-tech as you could get and still be broadcastable."

New Musical Express asked Byrne, "What sort of function do things like the 'Once In A Lifetime' video serve?" His response: "I wanted to make something that worked on its own, wasn't just a promo thing, didn't rely on the fact that it was a pop group or that you knew the song. Because it's always been thought that anything that's shorter than a half hour is just a promotional device for something else, a glorified ad for the record or the group — having very little value on its own, so the TV stations and the clubs get these things for free. They're helping you to sell your records — why should we pay you to show a three-minute ad? I think they're quite right about that, but some things might hold up on their own. But I'm not sure how that could be worked out, there might have to be a different category — something like the way the ASCAP and BMI and the performing rights societies work, so the TV stations and clubs pay a small fee every time they air something, the same way a radio station pays a small fee every time they play a

The Making of Remain In Light

record."

Although 'Once In A Lifetime' didn't hit within the Billboard 100 upon its release, it slowly caught on as people saw the video on MTV — the station played it in heavy rotation. Contrastingly, American radio wasn't as keen on supporting a single abundant in so many musical and cultural influences. Some stations even went so far as to regard the single as unplayable. "Talking Heads have never designed our music for radio air play," said Harrison in 1981. "Rather, we wanted to try and make what we considered interesting and, I guess, creative music. It was always sort of a gamble."

A live version of 'Once In A Lifetime', taken from the 1984 concert film *Stop Making Sense*, charted in 1985, reaching number ninety-one on the US Billboard Hot 100. Also, in 1986, when the latter version featured on *Down And Out In Beverley Hills*, it became widely known across generations and musical tastes — despite costing just fourteen-million dollars to make, the movie pulled in over sixty-million at the box office!

The rhythmic aspect of 'Houses In Motion' was inspired by reggae music. The chorus embraces a moment of call and response from Byrne and Eno. In the verses, Byrne's vocal style is almost anti-melodic.

'Houses In Motion' incorporates lengthy brass performances from Jon Hassell. The horn arrangements that come in towards the end of the song were written and performed by him. It features a trumpet that was played through a harmoniser. A similar extent of experimentation was embraced for the making of *Fourth World, Vol. 1: Possible Musics*.

An alternate mix of 'Houses In Motion' was released as a single in May 1981. The cover artwork for it was done by Thomi Wroblewski. It got to number fifty in the UK. On the B-side is 'Air' from *Fear Of Music*.

The twelve-inch remix of 'Houses In Motion' features an additional verse. The latter was included in live performances of the song. Talking Heads played 'Houses In Motion' as part of their live set right up until December 1983. A recording from November 1980 at the Emerald City club in Cherry Hill, New Jersey was included on their 1982 live album, *The Name Of This Band Is Talking Heads*.

'Seen And Not Seen' makes use of a spoken vocal line. The role of the rhythm section complements the story being told. *Melody Maker* considered in August 1981; "When you listen to him padding through the lyrics of 'Seen And Not Seen', you're listening to the pure, untreated voice of Byrne — thin, querulous, uncertain in pitch, but still chillingly precise."

'Seen And Not Seen' has a lot in common with The Velvet Underground's track, 'The Gift' from their 1968 *White Light/ White Heat* album. The latter features John Cale's deadpan reading of some prose that Lou Reed wrote while he was in college.

'Listening Wind' features Arabic music elements. Speaking of the track in later years, Chris Frantz described it as a "spooky song" and with having "a beautiful melody". The high-pitched guitar tones were performed by Adrian Belew. He achieved this by combining effects pedals with a guitar slide. A similar style of playing can be heard on his contribution to the 1981 King Crimson single, 'Matte Kudasai'.

Regarding the closing track of *Remain In Light*, 'The Overload', Chris Frantz spoke in later years of how the intention was to create a sound that matched what Talking Heads *thought* Joy Division would sound like. They had only read about the band and hadn't actually heard them before.

Credits

The question of who should be credited on the album — where and to what extent — was a point of tension, particularly after the recording was completed. Eno proposed that everybody

The Making of Remain In Light

who took part should nominate what percentage of each song the band members had written, the idea being that the final number would then be averaged to determine the split of royalties. In line with this, Eno asserted that he should be entitled to a sizeable proportion in view of the songwriting and playing that he'd done.

When given advanced copies of *Remain In Light*, it was an uncomfortable moment for Frantz, Harrison and Weymouth. The agreement had been that everyone would be credited in alphabetical order (David Byrne, Brian Eno, Chris Frantz, Jerry Harrison, and Tina Weymouth). Instead though, the credits were written as "music by David Byrne, Brian Eno and Talking Heads." It was a slap in the face for Frantz, Harrison and Weymouth, who were being treated like a mere backing band, despite having contributed to *Remain In Light* to the extent that they had.

Prior to that, Eno had wanted the front cover to say, "*Remain In Light* by Talking Heads and Brian Eno". This problem soon resolved itself though when it was agreed that because Eno didn't want to take part in the promotional tour for the record, it made sense to have only Talking Heads named on the cover of it.

Eno's production certainly brought something to the table that would have probably been notably absent otherwise. In particular, although the songs were born out of jam sessions, none of them go off at tangents that make the album feel like an overload of improvisation on the band's part. In fact, a vital aspect of *Remain In Light* is in Eno's use of production techniques. His process was centred on expression and spontaneity rather than wanting to get too bogged down with worrying about what the end product would sound like. In such regard, it could be said that *Remain In Light* was made in a way that was very much "in the moment". In later years, Eno compared the creative process to "looking out to the world and saying, 'What a fantastic place we live in. Let's celebrate it'."

On balance, from Byrne's point of view, having done a large proportion of the songwriting, he felt that being named on the record as an individual made sense in that regard. When asked if it annoyed him to be seen as the leader of Talking Heads, Byrne told *New Musical Express* in November 1980; "I enjoy it. I don't want it to get in the way of everybody being able to work together, but I certainly like getting recognition for what I've done."

Weymouth told *New Musical Express* in November 1980; "When we were discussing this record, Brian wanted to say it was *his* record, David wanted to say it was *his* record. They both thought it was the greatest venture of their lives... We all came in with different ideas of what we were going to do. It was the collective influences that created the result. No one could put an individual claim to it. Certainly we were listening to African records long before David and Eno were because Chris and I are into rhythm, and it's great rhythm, primarily. We turned them on to it. We'd already done that song 'I Zimbra' and I felt sure when we did that — we actually did two like that but 'Dub' didn't get onto the record — I felt sure that would be the direction of the next record. Plus, Eno had always said that he wanted to go into the studio cold with us, without any material, so that we could learn the way he makes albums, simple things layer upon layer. It's really not novel at all, it's just the old idea of jamming, one key, no chord changes. Everybody played and everybody produced. The songs were written by the five of us... It's not a big problem. I feel weird talking about it because it's like a family's dirty laundry, but it's not a huge conflict. David needs to have a lot of credit; that motivates him. And it's not a bitter thing."

Frantz added; "There's a mistake in the text of the first pressing of the record. On the next pressing the credits will read 'lyrics by Byrne with the exception of Byrne/Eno two songs, music by Byrne, Harrison, Frantz, Weymouth and Eno'. We just had to put our foot down and say, look, we don't just want to get paid a percentage or whatever because let's face it, I'm not worried about money. That's one of the luckier aspects of my life. Had I never been in Talking Heads I wouldn't be worried about money. It wasn't that, it was for the record. I wanted somebody to know that even if I didn't write a whole song I did make a contribution. It wasn't an administrative error; it was an error by a member of the band who is used to taking credit for everything that happens. And when it was put to him that this was not the right way to do things, he had to admit that it wasn't."

Overall, it was certainly the case that the debate surrounding how to credit the album was a source of difficulty for all concerned. Frantz said in later years, "we felt very burnt by the credits dispute."

Artwork

The idea for the album's artwork was conceived by Tina Weymouth and Chris Frantz with the help of Massachusetts Institute of Technology researcher Walter Bender and his ArcMac team (the precursor to the MIT Media Lab). Using the idea of *Melody Attack* as inspiration (the working title for *Remain In Light* was *Melody Attack* – named after a Japanese game show), Weymouth and Frantz created a collage of red warplanes flying in formation over the Himalayas. The planes are an artistic depiction of Grumman Avenger planes in honour of Weymouth's father, Ralph Weymouth, who was a US Navy admiral. The idea for the back cover included simple portraits of the band members. Weymouth regularly attended MIT throughout the summer of 1980. Whilst there, she worked with Bender's colleague, Scott Fisher, on the computer renditions of the ideas.

Talking Heads - *Remain In Light*: In-depth

Due to the limits of what the computers could do at the time, the process was a difficult one. The mainframe for the technology alone took up several rooms. Weymouth and Fisher used masks as the concept with which to experiment on the portraits. The faces — except for eyes, noses and mouths — of each band member were blotted out with blocks of red colour. Weymouth toyed with the idea of superimposing Eno's face on top of all four of Talking Heads' portraits as a means of being able to hint at what she thought of as his egotism.

The rest of the artwork — and the liner notes — were designed by Tibor Kalman and his company M&Co. Kalman offered his services for free. In the interest of creating further publicity, he even went so far as to discuss the use of unconventional materials such as sandpaper and velour for the LP sleeve. Weymouth, who was sceptical of hiring a design firm, insisted on sticking with the MIT computerised images.

It was during the process of designing the album art that Talking Heads decided against the title of *Melody Attack*, stating that it was "too flippant" in view of the music they'd recorded. It was from there that *Remain In Light* was adopted instead. Byrne explained, "Besides not being all that melodic, the music had something to say that at the time seemed new, transcendent, and maybe even revolutionary, at least for funk rock songs."

In response to the change of title, the image of the warplanes was relegated to the back of the sleeve and the doctored portraits became the front cover. Kalman later suggested that the planes were not removed altogether because they made a nod to the Iranian hostage crisis of 1979–81.

Weymouth advised Kalman that she wanted simple typography in a bold sans serif font. M&Co. implemented this and also came up with the idea of inverting the "A"s in "TALKING HEADS". Weymouth and Frantz decided to use the joint credit acronym of C/T for their contribution to the

The Making of Remain In Light

artwork. Bender and Fisher used initials and code names due to how the project was not an official MIT venture. As a result, the design credits read "HCL, JPT, DDD, WALTER GP, PAUL, C/T". Upon its release, *Remain In Light* was one of the first computer-designed LP covers.

The cover art certainly leant itself to any number of broad interpretations. *Music Player And Listener* considered of it in April 1981; "Those Heads are wearing face paint, those Heads are wearing techno-tribal masks."

Reception

Remain In Light was given its world premiere airing in its entirety on 10th October 1980 on WDFM radio station.

A track by the name of 'Unison' that was released on the reissue of *Remain In Light* didn't make it onto the original album. It featured as part of the radio advert for it though!

Not only was *Remain In Light* reviewed by many journalists but when it was, it was rare that any strongly negative comments were put forward about it (so much so that when researching for this book, no such things were encountered!). Of course, not everybody loved the album — that would simply be impossible! Still though, to be given such positive critical acclaim right across the board is rare for any album and in that regard alone, *Remain In Light* was exceptional. Clearly, it ticked a lot of boxes in terms of 1) bringing something different and innovative to the listener whilst 2) still managing to be catchy and memorable and thus, with commercial appeal. (Evidently, the reviewers didn't happen to come across one of the few faulty copies of *Remain In Light*; the fault being that side two featured the second side of the 1972 T. Rex album, *The Slider*).

All of the following reviews of *Remain In Light* were printed between October and December 1980:

From the *Santa Cruz Sentinel*: "Produced by avant-

Talking Heads - *Remain In Light*: In-depth

garde master Brian Eno, the new Talking Heads LP finds the band getting down to some very, very serious funk. Rhythms seemingly never heard before by man jump off this disc with Third World abandon, and the Heads succeed both commercially and artistically with an album destined to be a classic. Sassy horns and sidemen from sophistifunk superstars Parliament-Funkadelic add genuine touches of soulful, modern R&B to the Heads' already beat-crazy scheme. *Remain In Light* is maybe the best album of 1980, and that covers an awful lot of vinyl! Pick up this disc in time for Christmas. It'll shake the ornaments right off your tree."

The same publication said of the album a month later, "The Talking Heads have never been afraid to progress and they set themselves miles ahead of the rest in 1980 with *Remain In Light*, a fascinating collection of tunes which blend the urgency of rock 'n' roll with the mystery of unknown rhythms. Add David Byrne's highly intellectual songwriting, and you have one fine album."

From Pennsylvania's *Morning Call*: "'Lost my shape...' sings a giddy, yet confident, David Byrne on 'Crosseyed And Painless', one of his and mentor Brian Eno's best songs on Talking Heads' remarkable robust (not to mention groundbreaking) fourth LP. And anyone familiar with the Heads only from 'Psycho Killer' and 'Take Me To The River' will be thrown off guard (but ultimately won over) by this intriguing safari through the wilds of Afro-funk. Those who danced to 'I Zimbra' (from last year's first rate *Fear Of Music* LP) won't be so surprised. You may well wonder what four white kids are doing playing this kind of music. When I first heard about the Heads' performances at the Toronto new wave festival and a subsequent New York City gig in late August, I'll admit I had my misgivings. (I had visions of Byrne as a Lawrence Welk telling his Champagne Music Makers, 'play dat funky music, white boys!'). But *Remain In Light* rarely strikes a wrong note.

The Making of Remain In Light

('Listening Wind', while musically lovely and evocative, does have a sentimentalised theme: Western materialism polluting Third World simplicity). Like the good art school students they are, the Heads spent time studying African musical concepts, developing skills and attitudes before working in this genre. But most important, they use the steady melodic and rhythmic patterns to their own ends, always threatening to jump the groove, whether blowing hot ('Houses In Motion') or cool ('Seen And Not Seen'). The Heads are still idea-mongers too. There's a lot of talk about the shifting nature of things (the magical 'Once In A Lifetime' is my favourite) and the music reflects this by its sometimes random, atonal asymmetry. Without doubt, one of the year's best albums."

Referring to Talking Heads as "one of rock's most intriguing progressive bands," a Michigan paper said of *Remain In Light*; "If 'Life During Wartime' was to your liking, then the shuffling beat on *Remain In Light* will also attract you. Lyrically, David Byrne continues to create eerie visions with little connecting fibre from line to line. 'Seen And Not Seen' is a grabber, while the best listening is 'Crosseyed And Painless'. With their fourth album, Talking Heads keep breaking new ground. Proof that artistic integrity and ingenuity are far from dead in rock music."

As part of a feature titled, "Some New Releases Worth Hearing", *Remain In Light* was reviewed in New York's *Newsday*; "This New York-based band of former art students has abandoned conventional song structure in favour of African concepts, and at times, the results are tantalisingly hypnotic, with repeated rhythms constantly shifting in texture and tone. Lead singer David Byrne has shucked off much of his scared-kid sound. Now, when he sings of terror ('lost my shape, trying to act casual' in 'Crosseyed And Painless') he seems philosophical rather than paranoid, which I guess indicates a kind of maturity. But while some of the lyrics seem carefully calculated ('Seen And Not Seen' could stand on its own as a very short story), the randomness of others seems earnestly inane as anything by such sixties black holes as Ultimate Spinach and Earth Opera. And the shift of being jam-oriented (a number of outside musicians have joined the band) from its former song orientation deprives composer Byrne of the well-focussed balance between aesthetics and emotions that had made him New York's most intriguing songwriter. There's also the question of the influence of producer Brian Eno, who is co-author, with Byrne, of all the material. Despite the attractiveness of much of the record, one senses the imposition of Eno's own artistic theorems at the expense of Talking Heads' organic development."

The opinion expressed in the above is an interesting one in how it seems that the reviewer is basically saying something along the lines of "too many cooks spoil the soup". Really though, without Brian Eno — and indeed the additional musicians — in the equation, *Remain In Light* would have a different sound entirely (or would not exist at all!). So yes, it could be argued that Talking Heads could have gone in a different direction without bringing in extra people to work on their fourth album, but then, the scope to explore musically would have been, in some ways, less expansive.

Appreciating the music without musing on what may or may not have been, Canada's *Montreal Gazette* opined; "The most joyful, celebratory outpouring of Talking Heads' short career, this is an album about change, with the music in a constant state of flux. In a word, it's staggering."

From Iowa's *Gazette*: "Most of the new Talking Heads songs were built on top of layers of cross-rhythms, and the results sound something like black American funk or its African equivalent, Afro-Beat. But the Heads and their producer, Brian Eno, are more concerned with the philosophical ramifications of the holes left by displaced rhythms than they are with duplicating conventional dance grooves, and their orchestrated

The Making of Remain In Light

electronics and provocative verbal gambits are hardly standard funk fare. This is brave original music from a band that isn't afraid to keep growing."

From *The Courier News*: "It's often said that funky music relies too much on repetition. If that's so, it was only a matter of time before Talking Heads, champions of trance-rock, would explore it. Last year's *Fear Of Music*, with its Doors-like edge and full body was just a hint of this album's full-blown dance arrangements. The surface gloss makes the Heads sound more commercial than ever, but the edgy guitar lines and psychotic vocals are still there. As leader-songwriter David Byrne sang last album, 'This ain't no party...' and, if anything, his paranoid lyrics are more focused than ever. Take 'Once In A Lifetime': 'And you may find yourself...'. The ice cubes in the lyrics are offset by the warmth of the beat. This paradox is like the battle between the intellectual and emotional aspects of the self. And after years of coldness, it's good to know that the Heads understand that it's not all in the head."

From *The Tampa Bay Times*: "Because they approach them so pretentiously, the African rhythms and funk rudiments which Talking Heads appropriate here should disintegrate. That they don't is a tribute to the band's wonderful rhythm section as well as to the contemporary musicians added here. David Byrne's lyrics remain primarily opaque and more pompous than his approach to rhythm, but the way he chants them, letting fragments pop above the surface of the music, is also intriguing. I don't trust this, at least partly because it really believes that its sources are being "modernised", or maybe civilised is a better word. But it's comparatively listenable, and if you don't want to dance to it, you're missing the point."

From a Texas-based paper: "Colour this bunch ambitious. *Remain In Light* reaches for a remarkable fusion of black and white rock and often realises it. If you remember 'I Zimbra' from the Heads' last album, then imagine the same kind of

Talking Heads - *Remain In Light*: In-depth

intricate funk riffing stretched out and more densely textured. Always a band obsessed with rhythm, the Heads have rethought everything here in terms of funk. Each song is devoted to a single rhythmic pattern which is developed until its hypnotic effect — a dance trance if you will — takes over. The sound is thick and layered, with percussion, keyboards, and harmonies (by Brian Eno and Nona Hendryx, among others) added in large amounts, but it rarely sounds cluttered. However hard they are to decipher through the mix, Byrne and Eno's lyrics work superbly with the musical groove, as they are usually sung as a melodic counterpoint to the funk underpinnings. Byrne's favourite themes of anxiety and dislocation pop up as wild humour in 'Once In A Lifetime' and as abstract thoughts that turn into chants on 'Born Under Punches (The Heat Goes On)' and 'Crosseyed And Painless'. 'Seen And Not Seen', a sort of narrative about an Indian storing up supplies to use against white settlers, is more explicit and 'Listening Wind' contains some dazzling cinematic imagery. The major flaw this music suffers from is constricted, coiled up feeling that's striking at first but disappears on stage, where expansive warmth carries the day. If you saw Talking Heads perform recently then *Remain In Light* is almost demoted to the level of a concert memento. But only almost — what happens on this album is so far ahead of the pack it's hardly necessary to call it one of this year's best."

From California's *Fresno Bee*: "Clearly one of the most avant-garde musically interesting groups around is Talking Heads. *Remain In Light*, their latest venture, continues to break new ground in today's diverse musical society. Acid rock, disco and punk rock have all but ploughed under and buried for country rock, new wave and more R&B sounds. Now with Talking Heads we have a group which is more than willing to explore foreign lands — in this case, African-accented music. Here's a group whose sound, categorically-wise, is

The Making of Remain In Light

uncategorical. It's neither the familiar new wave, country rock, disco or R&B. *Fear Of Music*, their last album, dug into the funk and disco sound, but *Remain In Light*, the group's fourth and latest album, digs into an area of hard-packed ground, in which few have dug before. The musical intentions David Byrne — the group's leader — has, is simply to develop an understanding of African concepts. Byrne does this with statement; he's not compromising with any musical standard for the sake of commerciality. Musically, Byrne certainly doesn't compromise, instead he bravely explores. The four-member band moves in this direction by producing a more percussion-oriented style, with emphasis on rhythm over beat. The result is eight compositions based on endlessly repeated guitar-drum beats that resemble the basis of African music. In addition, Talking Heads travels even farther by adding guests such as Robert Palmer, Nona Hendryx and José Rossy to the album. Aside from that, the key or sometimes "fifth head" is producer/British musician Brian Eno. It's Eno and Byrne's compositions that are played on the album. Remaining band members include Chris Frantz, Jerry Harrison and Tina Weymouth. As part of the group's exploration, the musicians occasionally switched from their "assigned" instruments; where Byrne may play bass, Weymouth may play synthesiser. But in no way did this deter from the overall musical effect. Weaving through musical arrangements is a series of chants and recited phrases that emphasise the African accent. Excellent examples of this are 'Born Under Punches (The Heat Goes On)' and 'Crosseyed And Painless'. Despite a repetitive sound, the songs continue to surge ahead. Some interesting recited lyrics can be found on 'Once In A Lifetime'. There is only one song — 'The Overload' — that is so screeching and repetitively droning it should be shot and put out of its misery. Aside from that, the bulk of the album remains interestingly innovative and worth listening to."

From *The Muncie Evening Press*: "David Byrne and his

Talking Heads - *Remain In Light*: In-depth

Heads make up one of the new wave rock bands that should help keep the eighties on the move. With basic funky rhythms and melodic repetition woven together in a complex musical pattern, Talking Heads is different, indeed. Heads' music is not so much written as it is improvised — but it is polished and perfected after the improvisation."

From Washington's *Spokesman-Review*: "Talking Heads have turned their "fear of music" into a lust for rhythm. *Remain In Light* unlocks culture cages in order to abduct the wild and tamed rhythms of Africa, India, native America and black America. The rhythms mingle, mate, stack up, line up and generally don't stop. *Remain In Light* is — pardon the phrase — a rhythm orgy. Experimentation with rhythms of other cultures is as old as *Sgt. Pepper* (this year, it seems everybody is taking a reggae experiment to the science fair). But Heads songwriter David Byrne and songwriter-producer Brian Eno don't merely experiment with the lifeless cadavers of textbook beat patterns. Rather they jolt them with electricity until the dead bodies get up and dance. The Talking Heads have joined Peter Gabriel in this building-from-the-beat technique. But unlike Gabriel, they do it live as well as in the studio. For concerts, they beefed up their bony four-piece band with funk experts from the band Parliament-Funkadelic. From what I hear, the crowded stage creates an exciting concert. All I know is that the record grooves in my living room. (By the way, you may have to buy this album to hear the music. Although it's racing up the charts, local radio programmers are ignoring it). My biggest fear when I first heard about this album was that too much sound would drown David Byrne's unique lyrics. Thankfully, Byrne is back with more killers. The best examples are the songs 'Seen And Not Seen' — a devolved O. Henry story — and 'Once In A Lifetime', in which Byrne becomes Steve Martin as a trading Baptist preacher. I submit that Byrne is a humorist. Okay, so he's not Frank Zappa. But don't confuse his absurd urgency

The Making of Remain In Light

with seriousness. Behind the deadpan, David Byrne is smirking at those of us who take ourselves too seriously. For going all the way with a new idea while keeping the faith, I give the Heads three stars."

The Miami News considered of *Remain In Light*; "Granted, it takes more than a few listens to comprehend (and then appreciate and love) the reason these white New Yorkers are back — in black rhythms."

Listing *Remain In Light* as one of the best records of 1980, *The San Francisco Examiner* advocated of the album in the December; "Despite its upstart nature, new wave rock, for the most part, has yet to prove very experimental. At the forefront of American new wave since the beginning, Talking Heads took a daring commercial risk with this startling revision in the band's accepted sound. Adding David Bowie's old guitarist and a handful of veteran soul musicians, the Heads shaped the band into a kind of soul/punk fusion — cerebrofunk. Songwriter David Byrne retained his typically obtuse style, but the irresistible rhythms of the new sound gave his songs a throbbing pulse entirely different from previous Heads records. The rewarding results of this dramatic departure made *Remain In Light* one of this year's few recording surprises."

Cash Box reviewed it: "Whether you call it a wave or just modern music, the Talking Heads are at the forefront of it all. This time the pioneering foursome and guiding light/producer Brian Eno have concocted a heady brew that mixes Afro-funk and its neurotic, rhythmic, progressive sound. Chants, intricate percussion arrangements and an ever-so-funky back-up band help propel the Heads through their most adventuresome and stunning work yet. This ain't no disco, this ain't no party, this is music now for the future. For AOR."

From *New Musical Express*: "A memorandum from Byrne intended for the reviewing fraternity (I think) makes it clear that: 'This record is the product of the studio and interest in African

Talking Heads - *Remain In Light*: In-depth

rhythms and sensibilities.' Byrne goes on to explain that the album was prepared according to an improvisation framework, eschewing the practice of jamming and soloing in order to develop 'skills and attitudes... an understanding of African musical concepts, of interlocking and interdependent parts and rhythms.' The memorandum finishes by recommending a select bibliography of African related texts, themselves concomitant with the gist of NME's recent interview with Brian Eno. I was unable to secure these volumes over the weekend. Initial familiarity with the record has disappointed those people who locked onto *Fear Of Music* so readily; the new attitude seems to deliberately play down Talking Heads' evolving tension in favour of a broader, enigmatic and ambient funk — its hard core extracted over a selection of chants and barely modulated moods that have been par for Eno's course at least since the days of *Warm Jets* — and can readily be pinpointed by anyone familiar with the work of Miles Davis, Ornette Coleman and George Clinton on the one hand or Can, Berlioz and Wendy Carlos on the other. The implied raison d'être of the record, to strike a blow for high life timbres, falters on the grounds that more than ever Byrne and Eno are cracking the whips while our old pals, the Talking Heads, blend into the background along with an invited cast of technical experts, Adrian Belew, José Rossy, John Hassel. The subjugation of this personality is further proved by the band's recent live appearances where Bernie Worrell and Busta Cherry Jones (a long-time Eno associate) have been drafted in. Whither Jerry Harrison and Tina Weymouth in the current regime?"

"In fact a steadier appraisal of *Remain In Light* does uncover a host of hypnotic ideas, tentatively linked to Byrne's concept of guerrilla freedom fighters and government men overcome by their environment. The old monosyllabic textures of *Fear Of Music* have been transplanted into a smoother setting but even so, the sounds of the former band are recognisable eventually, bubbling against the primary colours of percussion and electronic treatment. The opening 'Born Under Punches (The Heat Goes On)' takes the fade of 'Life During Wartime' and 'I Zimbra' as a beginning with Byrne, exiled from some Graham Greene entertainment, intoning in his customary intelligent insane way. Meanwhile foreign bodies bleep and jump to the fore, approaching a strong funk that you last heard at length on 'One Nation Under A Groove'. Staying in the disco (with brains) is 'Crosseyed And Painless', a sublime synthesis of frothing rhythms (Fenders and drums), a cloying harmony from Eno and one of Byrne's engagingly tetchy monologues of the unwieldy nature of facts. 'The Great Curve', which closes side one, grapples with a potentially lethal exposition of African sensuality, finding the world on a woman's hips, anthropomorphic motions, listening to the earth beat. It's heady stuff that induces a pleasant surrender until Adrian Belew chips in with the record's only two traditional solos, both of them having more in common with rock and roll than is good for the track — though there can be no argument about the effect of the side as a whole. Talking Heads' psychedelic hovering musicians kick up a hedonistic dust storm that enthrals and excites just as surely as it doesn't go far enough to induce the intended sense of abandonment."

"Side two is made up of five related episodes, all of them linked to the power of the elements. Byrne's western terrorist persona is found questioning his domestic and financial values in light of the African experience. 'Once In A Lifetime' puts him in deep water, rather like Eliot's peaceful but very dead Phoenician, while Eno and the cast set up a Greek chorus of call and response, simulating the ocean blues and echoing snatches of 'Take Me To The River'. 'Houses In Motion' contrasts this simple permanence with the man on the move bereft of 'Style or grace... digging his own grave.' Byrne chants/talks this lyric over a building tempo of clavinet, formula funk guitars and

Talking Heads - *Remain In Light*: In-depth

John Hassel's ethereal horn arrangement. Your own body will tell you how good that feels. The spoken technique doesn't suit 'Seen And Not Seen' so immediately; the subject matter, concerning the ability to transform physical attributes by will power in order to take on another ideal appearance, may have some resonance for other cultures but its overtones of self obsession and pride are too cumbersome here to convince."

"The album's closing songs, 'Listening Wind' and 'The Overload', both of which make a substantial nod at Can's *Soon Over Babaluma*, are perhaps the most intriguing moments on a side of music which strips off its early dance rhythms and replaces them into a beautifully visual and cinematic context. 'Listening Wind' may be the most complex song that Byrne has yet written; it certainly stands as the pivotal point on what is undoubtedly a transitional record. The protagonist, a noble savage type who communes with the breeze, is fired with an instinctive desire to rid his locale (could be anywhere from Kinshasa to Phnom Penh) of the Yankee imperialists. The tone is strangely optimistic and sad at the same time, implying the death of those qualities which will eventually persuade the Third World nations to overthrow their oppressors (the strange rumblings in 'The Overload' are not just an uprising spirit). Without wishing to burden *Remain In Light* with any further critical lumber, it is obvious that Talking Heads, whatever they are now, have attempted something enterprising and fresh — the signposts are clear enough to direct them into new spaces. Given time to lower preconceptions and heighten senses, I found myself overtaken by an album of brave intentions and haunting textures. Safari, so good."

From *Record Mirror*: "Funk, the grand Afro-American dance tradition, and existentialism should be uneasy bedmates and probably are. Talking Heads glide over the problem this way: *Remain In Light* is Talking Heads' fourth album. The band arose at a time when the only contemporary countrymen

The Making of Remain In Light

in touch with modern dance were Tom Verlaine and his Television. These two units, strangely, considering America's lack of pioneering visionaries, moved to the front of the class. Verlaine is currently out in the playground, ready to return, and Talking Heads are still there. Jim Kerr of Simple Minds informed me recently that he had heard a track off *Remain In Light* on a French radio show. He described the track as true excellence and expressed the opinion that it made him want to give up there and then. I'd presume the track came from the first side of the album. Three tracks grace that side and the angle is Eno adulterated funk and a big band sound. Immediately I see Ken's point. With the Minds' latest, they explore bass and drum repetition in a pure dance medium; white neo-disco. The Heads become the lead white hopes on funk."

"'Born Under Punches (The Heat Goes On)' opens to much whooping and hollering before Byrne scat sings his way all over the choruses. Eno's involvement in the actual composition of the songs is apparent throughout, the signs being the Eno/Bowie/Sinatra romantically inflexed vocal lines that Byrne cuts through with on occasion. The groove winds into a haywire middle section that hurtles off in all directions over the still-solid rhythm and percussive backbeat. Then comes a masterful hook, a flowing repetition of the line 'Goes on and the heat goes on', while Byrne scat sings his way out. It's amongst the best of things you'll hear all year (what's left of it). Second cut 'Crosseyed And Painless' again pushes the bolting bass of Tina "let's go disco" Weymouth to the fore. Once more the groove rolls out with Byrne gibbering on about hospitals and related subjects. Again towards the end a new melody creeps in and the crew croon 'still waiting' over and over again. Third and most frantic with seven percussionists is 'The Great Curve', a number which tends toward salsa. Bongos a go-go with a horn section that cuts in and out with alarming severity and effect. Once more the beat seems to be of the utmost importance, leaving the gist of the lyrics largely incomprehensible. When the countermelodies mesh it makes things damn near impossible, in fact one feels sure that on this track the vocals are not English and are being employed as an extra instrument which conveys sound rather than any message or relevancies."

"Side two I'm less certain about. 'Once In A Lifetime' has Byrne delivering lyrics in asserted singspeak, questioning honest to goodness, American values (car, house, wife etc.). 'Houses In Motion' is really deep stuff. 'For a long time…' slurs Byrne with Dean/Brando/Kerouac young soul rebel sensibility. He continues: 'I knew my heart was in the right place…' What all that is about, I know not. 'Seen And Not Seen', whose handclaps are so weak they should've known better, is Byrne lecture. Pure twaddle, spoken not sung, it deals in the Kafka, or is it Sartre-esque trials of a man who wills his face into the ideals he sees in mags and the movies. He ends, of course, by eternally questioning his decision. The groove seems to have been written to accommodate the short story and is the weaker because of it. 'Listening Wind' by comparison is beautiful. The story, as far as I can ascertain, of American expansion, it tells the story of Mojique who watches the Americans, whom he serves from the hills. The chorus instils feelings of the Red Indian tribal unity with talk at the wind; friend guide and the power that will drive them away. Masterful, and it sets the mood for 'The Overload' — a fat moody overtly Eno number that utilises one not sustained to the full and sounds like it employs the Bowie cut up lyric writing method. 'Gentle collapsing of every surface…'. All too abstract for this meat-and-two-veg man, I'm afraid. Despite initial reservations this shows that Talking Heads — when Eno lays back a bit — are still a neck ahead. Nice to see that The Associates and The Simple Minds are the boys snapping at their heels though. Side one I suspect is more Byrne and band, and side two is more Eno. Side one is great music, side two is for the most part, good music. The choice is theirs and they've made it. Meanwhile I can only fantasise about a Talking Heads album produced by Rodgers and Edwards (Chic) or George Clinton. Until then though, Heads, they win."

From *Melody Maker*: "*Remain In Light* might be described as a collection of songs for life during the wartime David Byrne anticipated on *Fear Of Music*. Certainly, these are songs in which the dreadful has already happened, in which disaster and alarm have an almost *physical* presence. Byrne's first songs for Talking Heads mostly focused on moments of private crisis and panic; small moments of personal terror, minor irrationalities, absurd fears beyond which lurked a larger madness. On *Remain In Light* that madness is more public. The tears in the fabric of normality, previously hinted at, are more vividly exposed. Byrne's writing has *grown*. The best moments in his songs are still those which illuminate crucial details of personalities cracking and collapsing, but his basic themes are now more impressively expansive, talking in not only individual aberrations but international breakdowns: American colonialism, government murders, revolution, and on 'The Overload' society's imminent collapse. Talking Heads' music has grown too: away from the taut structures of the first two albums, in pursuit of directions suggested by 'I Zimbra'. Another direct influence on the musical shape of *Remain In Light* might be Fripp's notion of discotronics as expressed on 'Under Heavy Manners', to which Byrne contributed."

"'Born Under Punches (The Heat Goes On)', the expanded opening track here, is directly reminiscent of 'Manners', with its gibbering guitars and keyboards cross-hatched over a snapping disco beat and Byrne's traumatised vocal ('Take a look at these hands!' he shrieks for openers) recalling his mind-bending intro to the Fripp album. The track sprawls all over the shop, accommodating innumerable musical and vocal intrusions and enough percussion effects to furnish a psychotic fiesta. Lyrically, it's vague (to say the least). But enough information emerges to suggest it's a kind of dislocated portrait of a government assassin (there's a line about 'falling bodies tumbling across the floor'). Musically, it's amongst the most striking things Talking Heads have done, especially memorable for the dazzling vocal arrangements that are a characteristic of the album and reach some kind of bewildering apotheosis on 'The Great Curve'. 'Crosseyed And Painless' again zeroes in on a state of mental distress, more forcefully than anything else in Byrne's repertoire. Byrne screams above the venomously chopping guitars and Chris Frantz' unswerving snare drum crack. Eno's alien falsetto backing vocal questions and comments upon the narrator's predicament. 'There was a time, there was a formula', he swoons with enlightening poise. Side one bows out with the seven-minute rhythmic crash of 'The Great Curve' which has Byrne and Jerry Harrison exchanging terse guitar phrases, sharp, stabbing horns, massive collisions of vocal tracks, including an extraordinary doo-wop section wailing continuously. Byrne remains frozen front and centre, trying to make sense of it all before being blown away by former Bowie sideman Adrian Belew's coruscating guitar strafing."

"'Once In A Lifetime' opens side two, with Byrne setting a worried, fatigued present against the romantic possibilities of an idealised past. The result is as poignant as Springsteen's 'The River' (which attempts the same trick), but less sentimental, more harrowing. It also features the album's most gloriously melodic chorus. 'Houses In Motion' is the record's masterpiece, a brilliantly realised evocation of the urban menace redolent of one of Travis Bickle's neurotic monologues in *Taxi Driver*. Byrne drawls with sinister glee over a sombre, aggressive rhythm. 'Seen And Not Seen' is as mordant, but suffused in bizarre humour, with drumbeats and handclaps and a discreet melodic chorus punctuating Byrne's narrative about a man who assumes the facial characteristics of

The Making of Remain In Light

people he sees in magazines, on TV and in the movies. If the songs have so far been examinations of interior collapse, the final pair, 'Listening Wind' and 'The Overload', anticipate the final disaster Byrne appears to believe is inevitable. 'Listening Wind' is a beautifully constructed piece, enhanced by a swirling melody, that celebrates the spirit of rebellion in the Third World (the lyrics could apply to South America, Africa or Indochina) and decries American imperialism. 'The Overload' takes the album out with the awful force of Costello's 'Night Rally' and the sonorous momentum of Joy Division. 'Terrible signals, too weak to even recognise,' Byrne laments, resigned to the end. Few albums this year have taken on so much as *Remain In Light*; no rock album since *Station To Station* has sounded so radical without deserting the mainstream it has to occupy if it's to be heard."

From *Rolling Stone*: "Seldom in pop music history has there been a larger gap between what black and white audiences are listening to than there is right now. While blacks are almost entirely uninterested in the clipped, rigid urgency of the new wave, it's doubtful that more than a small percentage of *Rolling Stone*'s predominantly white readership knows anything at all about the summer's only piece of culture-defining music, Kurtis Blow's huge hit, 'The Breaks'. Such a situation is both sad and ironic, because rarely have the radical edges of black and white music come closer to overlapping. On one hand, the gang of four utilise their bass guitar every bit as prominently and starkly as the curt bass figures that prod the spoken verses in 'The Breaks'. On the other, Chic producers Nile Rodgers and Bernard Edwards choose to make Diana Ross sound as sullen and alienated as Deborah Harry. None of this has escaped the notice of Talking Heads, however, and *Remain In Light* is their brave, absorbing attempt to locate a common ground in today's divergent, often hostile musical community. From the first, Talking Heads' contribution to the avant-punk scene they

Talking Heads - *Remain In Light*: In-depth

helped create was their emphasis on rhythm over beat. While the Ramones' rockers banged and Blondie's blared, the Heads' early songs pulsed, winding their way past jitteriness to achieve the compelling tension that defined a particular moment in rock and roll history — a moment when white rock fans wanted to dance so badly, and yet were so intimidated by the idea, that they started hopping straight up and down for instant relief. By 1978, punk and disco had divided the pop audience. What did Talking Heads do? They recorded Al Green's 'Take Me To The River'. The gesture was a heroic one. Despite David Byrne's vocal restraint and certain puritanical tendencies in his lyrics to value work over pleasure ('Artists Only', 'Don't Worry About The Government'), Talking Heads never stopped learning from the sensuous music that existed in a world parallel to theirs. On 1979's *Fear Of Music*, they made a defiant connection with funk and disco in 'I Zimbra' and 'Life During Wartime', both of which aid in preparing us for *Remain In Light*'s startling avant-primitivism."

"On *Remain In Light*, rhythm takes over. Each of the eight compositions adheres to a single guitar-drum riff repeated endlessly, creating what funk musicians commonly refer to as a groove. A series of thin, shifting layers is then added: more jiggly percussion, glancing and contrasting guitar figures, singing by Byrne that represents a sharp and exhilarating break with the neurotic and intentionally wooden vocals that had previously characterised all Talking Heads albums. Though the tunes take their time (side one has just three cuts), nobody steps out to solo here. There isn't any elaboration of the initial unifying riff either. Because of this, these songs resemble the African music that the band has taken great pains to acknowledge as *Remain In Light*'s guiding structure."

"An even bolder example of the African influence is *My Life In The Bush Of Ghosts*, an LP recorded by David Byrne and Brian Eno that may never be issued in its ideal form. *My*

The Making of Remain In Light

Life In The Bush Of Ghosts uses fixed staccato rhythm patterns in much the same way that Eno's early solo work built whole compositions around simple synthesiser clusters. In place of formal singing, the album substitutes "found" vocals: e.g., random voices taped off the radio. Indeed, one of these voices, that of evangelist Kathryn Kuhlman, threw the entire project into legal limbo with a threat to sue unless it was removed. Sire has indicated that the disc will probably be remixed, but no release date has been set. Which is too bad, because *My Life In The Bush Of Ghosts* enhances the aesthetic of *Remain In Light*, and at least one of its sections, 'Shaking With My Voice', is as strange and thrilling a piece of music as either Byrne or Eno has ever made."

"In addition to its African influences, *Remain In Light* also flashes the ecstatic freedom of current American funk, across which any number of complex emotions and topics can roam. In both 'Born Under Punches (The Heat Goes On)' and 'Crosseyed And Painless', the rhythm lurches about while always moving forward, thrust ahead by the tough, serene beat of the bass and percussion. Throughout, instruments are so tightly meshed that it's often difficult to pick out what you're hearing — or even who's playing. As part of their let's-rethink-this-music attitude, Talking Heads occasionally play one another's instruments, and guests as disparate as Robert Palmer and Nona Hendryx are enlisted. (By now, of course, producer Brian Eno can be considered a fifth Head.) Far from being confusing, however, such density contributes greatly to the mesmerising power exerted by these elaborate dance tunes."

"Though you can follow, to some extent, the story lines of, say, 'Listening Wind' (in which an Indian stores up weaponry to launch an assault on plundering Americans) and the spoken fable, 'Seen And Not Seen', *Remain In Light*'s lyrics are more frequently utilised to describe or embody abstract concepts. Thus, beneath the wild dance patterns of 'Crosseyed And

Painless', there lurks a dementedly sober disquisition on the nature of facts that culminates in a hilarious, rapidly recited list of characteristics ('Facts are simple and facts are straight...') that could go on forever — and probably does, since the song fades out before the singer can finish reading what's on the lyric sheet. Elsewhere, strings of words convey meaning only through Byrne's intonation and emphasis: his throaty, conspiratorial murmur in 'Houses In Motion' adds implications you can't extract from lines as flyaway as 'I'm walking a line — I'm thinking about empty motion'."

"In all of this lies a solution to a problem that was clearly bothering David Byrne on *Fear Of Music*: how to write rock lyrics that don't yield to easy analysis and yet aren't pretentious. Talking Heads' most radical attempt at an answer was the use of da-daist Hugo Ball's nonsense words as a mock-African chant in 'I Zimbra'. The strategy on *Remain In Light* is much more complicated and risky. In compositions like 'Born Under Punches' and 'Crosseyed And Painless', phrases are suggested and measured, repeated and turned inside out, in reaction to the spins and spirals of their organising riff-melodies. At no time does the music change to accommodate the completion of a conventional pop-song sentiment or clever line. Once in a while, the experiments backfire on the experimenters. Both 'The Great Curve' and 'The Overload' are droning drags, full of screeching guitar noise that's more freaked-out than felt. Usually, however, the gambler's aesthetic operating within *Remain In Light* yields scary, funny music to which you can dance and think, think and dance, dance and think, ad infinitum."

The Making of Remain In Light

ON THE ROAD

Talking Heads / The Beat

Greek Theatre, Los Angeles

No fear of funk

THIS WAS no more toe-tapper. We're talking worn shoe-leather tonight, holes in the soles and corns on the toes, sore feet in a venue more used to producing sore behinds with its no-dance policy. Two and a half hours of solid bop with barely a half hour off for cocktails.

Single male ear-rings jangling in the aisles, satin jacketed execs kicking their Gucci boots up to their beards, journalists tapping their notebooks in time to contagious rhythms. The English Beat ("English" so as not to be confused with a similarly-tagged quartet of mop-top American Knack-sters) shared the calluses forming with a hint with that belied reports of bitchy live performances from earlier on this tour, and that managed to jam about fit their entire repertoire into the short allotted time.

The rhythm was spot on, the singing perfect and the sound so good it almost drifted the speakers. A couple of minutes of pure beat burning into your brain then bursting onto the next one, linked by some wild onstage bopping. 'Tears Of A Clown' stood out because just about everyone knew it, 'Mirror In The Bathroom' and 'Hands Off She's Mine' stood out because they're so damn good. A standing ovation; no less, brought them back for one more minute of 'Click Click' (seemed just can't be encored at the Greek Theatre). Make an entirely furore in the best-repair counter.

Talking Heads are being called "intellectual funk", dunno know, by people who won't raise their feet without raising their consciousness. Come on! Foo could always dance to most of the Heads' stuff, with or without strange drugs, only now it seems it's officially-kind to do so. Black and white music have been effectively reigned by this brainy bunch so you can gulfdashy have fun.

The sound is big, monstrous, captivating Parliament-Funka-delic with down-to-earth solid rhythms and eerie, dreamy flourishes, smooth melodies and a beat so tight and unignorable as well stacked new leather pants. The overall sound effect is more African than Kunta Kinte. The only one of the nine — yes nine: they used to be three, then four, now it's like a Sen Har set-up there with a Parl-Funk keyboardist, a Bowie guitarist, an ex LaBelle chantreuse; you've got to move with the changes — who didn't have black roots showing was Tina Weymouth (newly virginal look with long blonde hair, long dress, bare feet, pale smile, mixes well with him, strong bass playing). Things ain't what they used to be.

Lots off the new album sandwiched between 'Psycho Killer' as the first number and 'Take Me To The River' at the end. And even these have new improved versions, funked up along with the other couple of older numbers in the middle to a new upbeat, almost deliciously jaunty level. The Afro-pop beat just sort of happens, one song pretty much drifting in and out of the others, verdelissed by the odd jagged buzzsaw guitar, twitchy percussion or sharp, nervy synthesiser, but otherwise just slinking and pulsating and growing along like all good funk should, building up momentum with each rhythm.

And David Byrne, Gadfrum, almost nutty, opens his mouth wide like a choirboy and out comes soul. Gone (well almost) is the high-voice squeaky little psycho of old, and instead we have a soul singer. Okay so he doesn't soul roses into the audience and throw kisses a lot, but he does growl and hoo and wiggle his legs and grin and do clumsy dances (as opposed to Dolette McDonald's sensual writhes) and he does seem to be happy with the metamorphosis.

He smiles a lot of the time, trading vocals quite nicely with McDonald's, most admirably on 'River' but just as impressively elsewhere. The cast of thousands system really seems to work for them. The best (other than those mentioned already) were a slinky dance tune 'Houses In Motion', 'Crosseyed And Painless', 'Life During Wartime', and almost discoey 'Cities' (though the weren't so disco: the unchanging white light made the stage look more like the Braille Institute arranged the lighting). The devotees upped and danced throughout, though several spent each small gap between songs calling for old favourites, and many seemed to be hearing 'Remain In Light' for the first time.

This is definitely the sort of music I'd like to hear in airports, dazos or anywhere else for that matter. There's something about these skinny blokes with high voices — even when they're doing their best to keep them low and fat and funky.

SYLVIE SIMMONS

TINA WEYMOUTH models new virginal look

Talking Heads - *Remain In Light*: In-depth

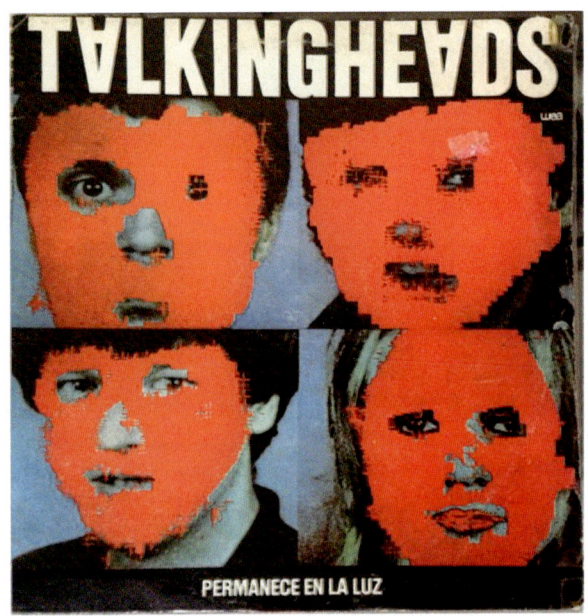

Argentina

Japan

The cover design remained consistent in all territories. There were slight variations in some cases though. In Argentina, the album title was in Spanish. In Japan, the album came with the usual obi, providing details in Japanese.

USA

South Africa

Like the cover, the Sire label design was fairly uniform in all the countries where *Remain In Light* was released on that label. In some countries though, the album was released on Warner Bros (Sire's parent label). In Greece, it was issued on WEA.

Yugoslavia

Greece

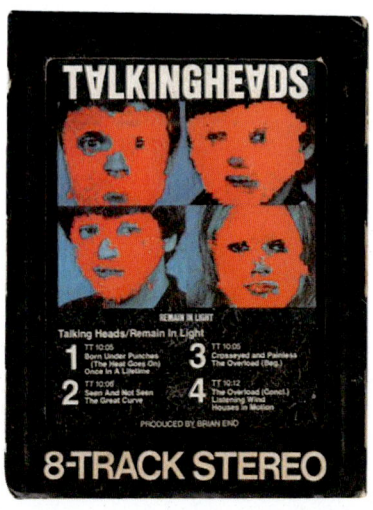

The album was also released on 8-track in the States.

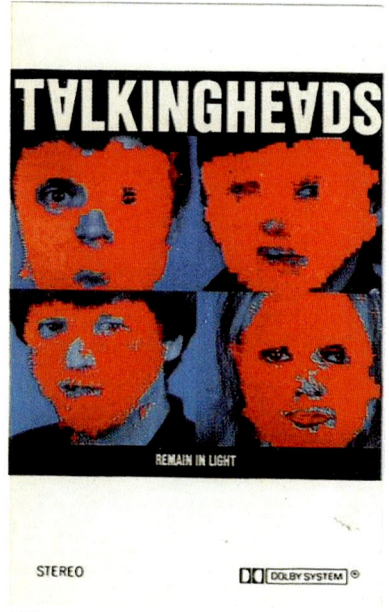

UK

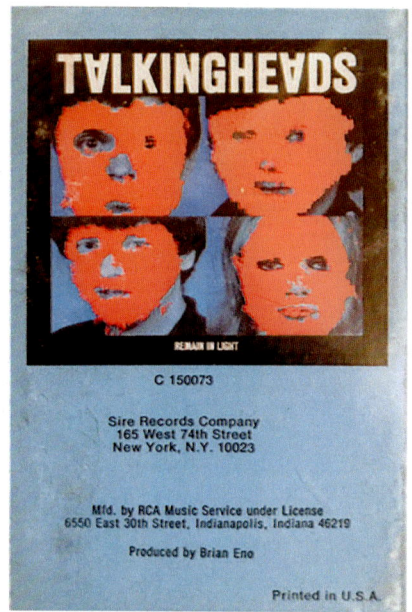

USA club edition

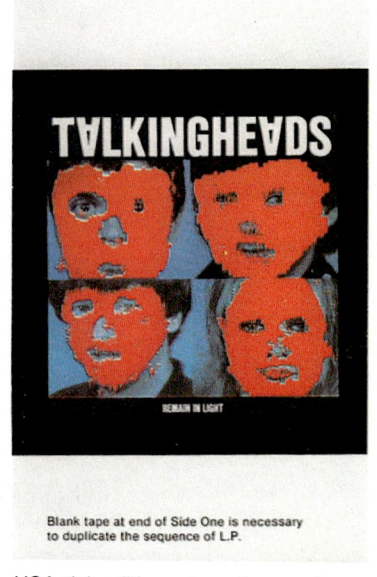

USA club edition, alternative version

The cassette format provided many variations with the square cover having to fit into a rectangular format.

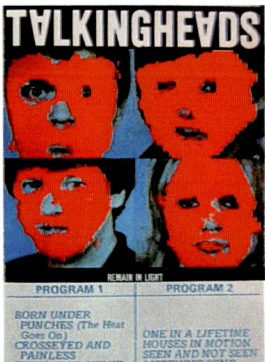
Canada

Japan

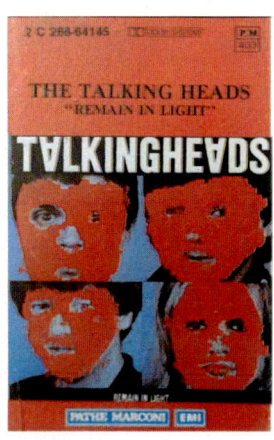
France

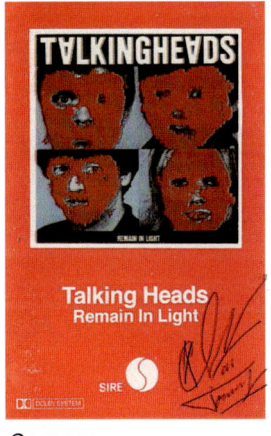
Germany

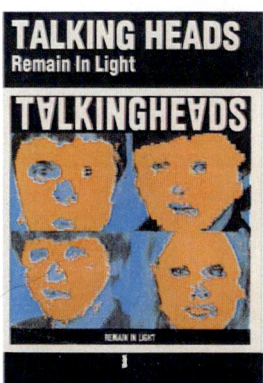
Germany reissue

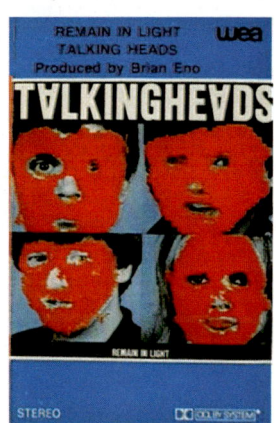
Greece

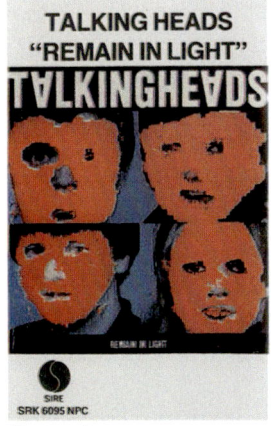
Portugal

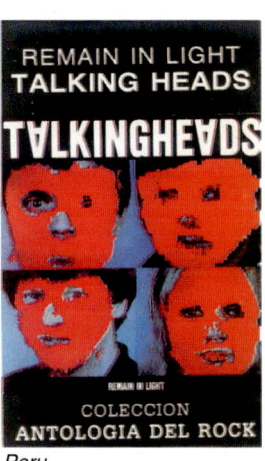
Peru

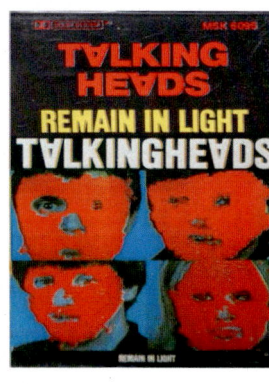
Australia

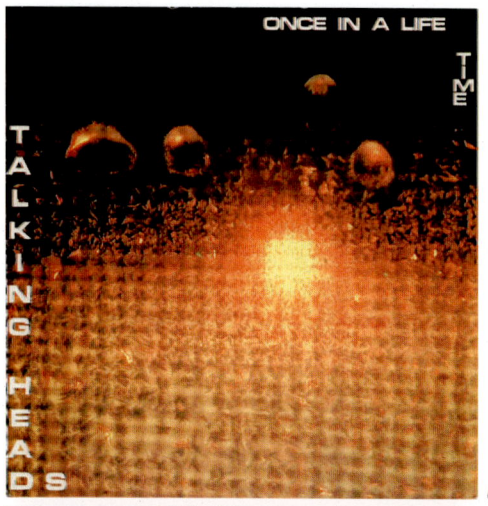
UK

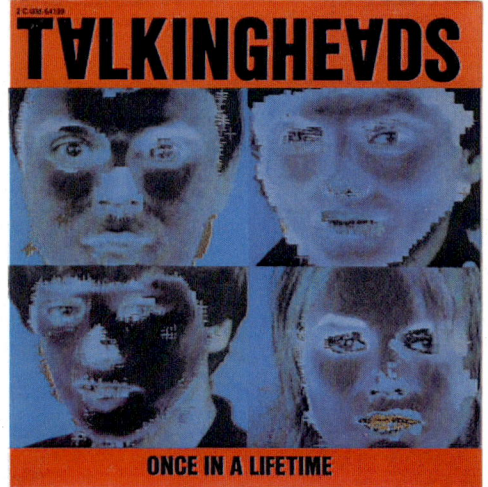
France

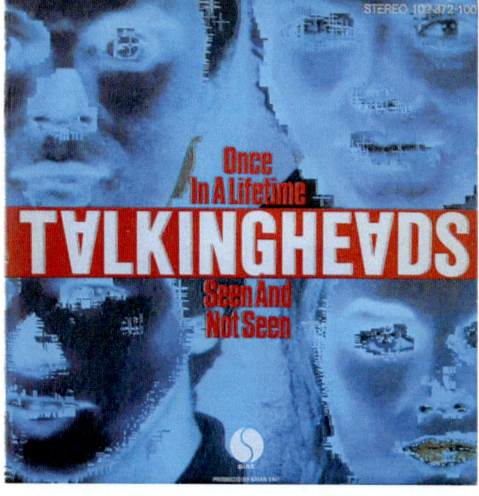
Germany

There were plenty of different sleeve designs for the 'Once In A Lifetime' single.

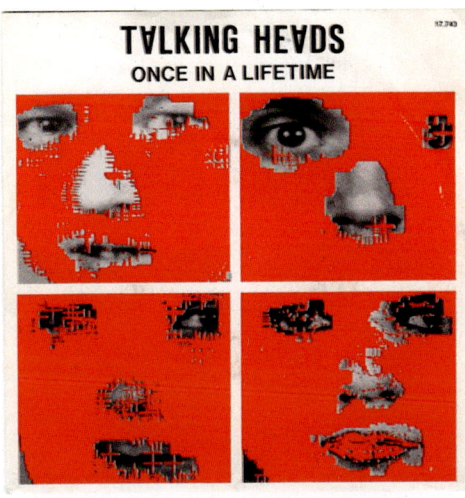

Benelux

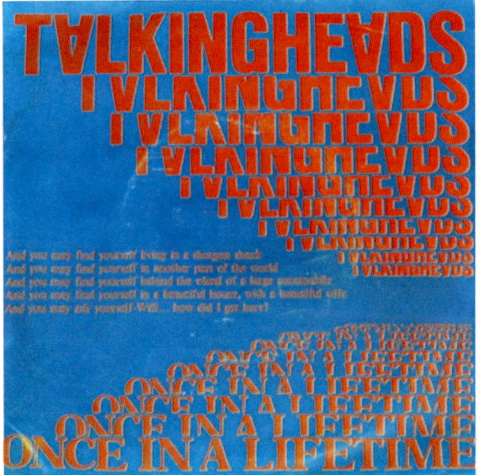

Portugal

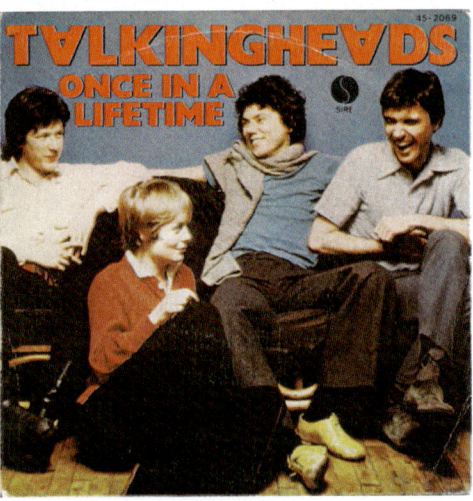

Spain

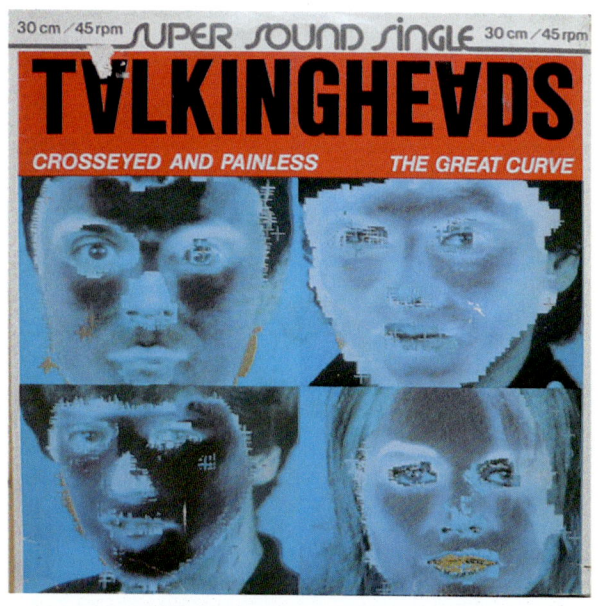

In Germany 'Crosseyed And Painless' was released as a 12" single.
'Born Under Punches (The Heat Goes On)' was released in Japan.

Chapter Three

The Tour

Album sales were boosted by the success of the tour. For the live performances, Talking Heads opted to bring in more musicians. It was considered a necessary move in view of the complexities made in the studio that needed to be performed on stage. Harrison was tasked with assembling the expanded line-up. It consisted of Bernie Worrell from Parliament-Funkadelic joining on keyboards, Adrian Belew on second guitar, Busta Jones as a second bass player, Steve Scales adding percussion and Dolette McDonald on backing vocals.

Harrison told *New Musical Express* in November 1980; "Really, the band that we have now is the result of the work I did with other people. I had met Busta Jones and he called me up to play with The Escalators. Then we went down to Philadelphia and I produced some demos for Nona Hendryx. I started moving around that scene in New York. I met Bernie Worrell through Busta — he played on Busta's album on Spring Records. Dolette had sung on The Escalators album. Steve Scales, I didn't know. We found him through Bernie. And Adrian Belew we met when he was recording in New York with David Bowie."

It was Eno who advised Talking Heads that the music on *Remain In Light* was too demanding for a quartet to perform live. To prepare for the tour, the nine-piece band did soundchecks in Frantz and Weymouth's loft. They referred to rhythmic ideas that had been established by Worrell, who had studied at the New England Conservatory and Juilliard School.

Talking Heads - *Remain In Light*: In-depth

In November 1980, *New Musical Express* considered of the expanded line-up; "The result is a nine-piece Talking Heads, lush instead of brittle. It's probably the single most radical step so far in the progress of America's so-called premier new wave band. Even a new wave band has to move with the times. Talking Heads have finally gone two-tone! Eleven months ago, when they played the last date of their tour in London, the group was on the verge of apoplexy. They had been touring eight months out of the year for the previous four and were almost wrung out with the routine. The working methods and approaches they had learned with Brian Eno had kept them fresh and stimulated in the studio and produced a consistent evolution on record, but on stage they had ground to a halt. They needed a new edge. Animated drum podiums and laser lights were not the answer."

So, what sort of audience did the tour engage? In response to the journalist's comment that "the white rock audience and the black soul audience rarely overlap in this country," Byrne told *New Musical Express* in November 1980; "That's true. I think for our audience, considering the kinds of groups they might go to see, we're a real exception. When we put the group together we didn't think of that, but it was obvious when it happened. We just chose the kind of musicians that happened to be the most appropriate to what we were doing. Actually it's more than happened to be; a lot of it's in the nature of the sensibility implied in that music."

In response to the journalist's comment that Talking Heads had always been a funky band, Byrne said; "Yeah, there's precedents for it in our previous stuff. But in the moments when this group really works, the underlying sensibility is very different from what it was before, a real radical shift. This music, when it really comes together right, has a transcendent feeling, like a trance of some sort. That's exactly what happens in traditional African music and other Third World music. It's something that isn't sought after in most pop music. We're aiming for something different, although some of the elements may be the same. When it works you get the feeling: forget yourself and become part of the community. It's wonderful and doesn't happen every night."

Although some of the bootlegs suggest that there were perhaps occasional variations in the setlist, overall, the following was pretty much the standard:

Psycho Killer
Warning Sign
Stay Hungry
Cities
Band intros
I Zimbra
Drugs
Once In A Lifetime
Animals
Houses In Motion
Born Under Punches
Crosseyed And Painless
Life During Wartime
Encore one: Take Me To The River
Encore two: The Great Curve

On the 23rd August 1980 when Talking Heads performed at the Heatwave Festival in Canada, it was the first time that they did so with the expanded line-up. A journalist wrote; "The Talking Heads appear to know the crowd, as at least 50,000-strong have made a special effort to be here. The Talking Heads have come prepared to fully reward that effort. This is the premier of a new version of the band as mastermind David Byrne has extended the band's line-up. He's brought in the hired guns; the rock and roll hitmen. The band on the stage includes bassist Busta Jones, keyboardist Bernie Worrell of Parliament-

Talking Heads - *Remain In Light*: In-depth

Funkadelic fame, vocalist Dolette McDonald; percussionist Steven Scales, and a David Bowie alumni — Adrian Belew, plus the original core members. They open with a perfunctory performance of 'Psycho Killer'. Then the magic begins. The music is as full and as succinct as David Byrne's early creations have always promised. The songs from *Fear Of Music* and the new compositions are euphoria-inducing performed live: fine rushes up and down your spine — alpha waves — funk waves — please-don't-let-it-ever-stop waves — take some risks, stay-true-to-your-heart and you-might-go-to-heaven waves. The Talking Heads throw down the musical gauntlet with easily the outstanding performance of the festival."

Other sources have stated that the Heatwave Festival attracted a crowd of 70,000 people. The *Los Angeles Times* described Talking Heads' performance there as a "rock-funk sound with dramatic, near show-stopping force."

Performing to large audiences was a commonality across the entire Remain In Light tour. On 27th August the band performed to a full house of 8,000 at the Wollman Rink. At New York City's Central Park, they played to a crowd of approximately 10,000 who were seated on the grass outside the walls. The Canada and New York dates were the only ones that had been planned. Sire Records soon decided to support the nine-member band on an extended tour though.

In November 1980, *Sounds* reviewed the performance that took place at the Greek Theatre in Los Angeles; "This was no mere toe-tapper. We're talking worn shoe leather tonight, holes in the soles and corns on the toes, sore feet in a venue more used to producing sore behinds with its no dance policy. Two and a half hours of solid bop with barely a half hour off for cocktails. Single male earrings jangling in the aisles, satin-jacketed execs kicking their Gucci boots up to their beards, journalists tapping their notebooks in time to the contagious rhythms... Talking Heads are being called "intellectual funk",

The Tour

don'tcha know, by people who won't raise their feet without raising their consciousness. Come on! You could always dance to most of the Heads' stuff, with or without strange drugs, only now it seems it's officially cool to do so. Black and white music have been effectively bridged by this brainy bunch so you can guiltlessly have fun. The sound is big, monotonous, captivating punkadelic with down-to-earth solid rhythm and eerie dreamy flourishes, smooth melodies and a beat as tight and unignorable as well-stacked new leather pants. The overall sound effect is more African than Kunta Kinte. The only one of nine — yes nine; they used to be three, then four, now it's like a *Ben-Hur* set up there with a Parliament-Funkadelic keyboardist, a Bowie guitarist, you've got to move with the changes — who didn't have black roots showing was Tina Weymouth (newly virginal look with long blonde hair, long dress, bare feet, pale smile; mixes well with hot, strong bass playing). Things aren't what they used to be."

"Lots of the new album sandwiched between 'Psycho Killer' as the first number and 'Take Me To The River' at the end. And even these have new improved versions, funked up along with the other couple of older numbers in the middle to a new upbeat, almost deliriously jaunty level. The Afro-pop beat just sort of happens, one song pretty much drifting in and out of the others, vandalised by the odd jagged buzzsaw guitar, twitchy percussion or sharp, nervy synthesiser, but otherwise just slinking and pulsating and grooving along like all good funk should, building up momentum with each rhythm. And David Byrne, deadpan, almost nutty, opens his mouth wide like a choirboy and out comes *soul*. Gone (well, almost) is the high-voice squeaky little psycho of old, and instead we have a soul singer. Okay so he doesn't toss roses into the audience and throw kisses a lot, but he does growl and bop and wiggle his legs and grin and do clumsy dances (as opposed to Dolette McDonald's sensual writhes) and he does seem to be happy with the metamorphosis. He smiles a lot of the time, trading vocals quite nicely with McDonald, most admirably on 'River' but just as impressively elsewhere."

"The cast-of-thousands system really seems to work for them. The best (other than those mentioned already) were a slinky dance tune 'Houses In Motion', 'Crosseyed And Painless', 'Life During Wartime' and almost discoed 'Cities' (though this weren't no disco; the unchanging white light made the stage look more like the Braille Institute arranged the lighting). The devotees upped and danced throughout, though several spent each small gap between songs calling for old favourites, and many seemed to be hearing *Remain In Light* for the first time. This is definitely the sort of music I'd like to hear in airports, discos or anywhere else for that matter. There's something about these skinny blokes with high voices — even when they're doing their best to keep them low and fat and funky."

Cash Box also reviewed a performance that took place at the Greek Theatre (it is unclear as to whether it was the same performance as the one reviewed in *Sounds*; Talking Heads played at this venue on the 17th and 18th October 1980): "David Byrne has gotten out his chemistry set once again and developed the latest catalyst in modern music. Byrne and his Talking Heads have long been extollers of the intellectual urban sound within the new wave, but on the new *Remain In Light* LP, the band and producer Brian Eno have merged the "think" with the funk. And what's more, the group's new pioneering sound, which weds Parliament-Funkadelic and traditional African rhythms with heady avant wave stylings, can be reproduced on stage. The celebrated New York band's recent gig at Los Angeles' Greek Theatre was proof positive of this phenomenon, as professor Byrne and his new expanded group worked their multi-ethnic sound experiment on a stunned Angelino audience and came up with a new scientific breakthrough."

The Tour

"The original quartet (Byrne, Harrison, Weymouth and Frantz) opened the show with its hypnotic anthem 'Psycho Killer'. Then the band slipped into its new African groove with 'I Zimbra' and by the time it bounded into the new *Remain In Light* material, the funk machine had been assembled and was in full swing. The expanded band featured an additional keyboardist (Parliament-Funkadelic's Bernie Worrell), guitarist (Bowie crony Adrian Belew) and bassist (funk master Busta Jones), a percussionist (Steven Scales) and a female vocalist (Gospel-oriented Dolette McDonald) and it metamorphosised the basic core of ex-architecture students into a throbbing juggernaut of a dance band."

"Songs such as 'Animals', 'Life During Wartime' and the thunderous 'Take Me To The River' were so embellished by the Afro-funk sound that they carried the fervour of a tribal dance. And the whole ensemble was clearly under the guidance of mastermind Byrne, who, judging from his random growls and flopping body movements, was ecstatic at the results of his latest sound project. Although it seemed that the funk machine was fragile and could break down at any moment, this inspired team broke through both the sound and culture barrier with its 'Once In A Lifetime' creation while at its Greek Theatre gig. For the time being, it had concocted a music that could please new-wavers and funk fans alike, and place one nation under a groove."

A lucky fan who was there for the two London dates that Talking Heads did in December 1980 (1st and 2nd) spoke of how due to the band's output of previous years, tickets were in great demand. Not only did Talking Heads have a steady track record of putting out a strong LP every year since 1977, but there were only two UK shows included as part of their European leg of the Remain In Light tour.

Talking Heads had first toured the UK as a support act to the Ramones (both bands had played at CBGB in the earlier

Talking Heads - *Remain In Light*: In-depth

Double Talking

THE TALKING HEADS (above) play two dates in London early in December as part of a European tour. They play Hammersmith Palais on December 1 and move over the road to play Hammersmith Odeon on the 2nd. Tickets for the Palais are £3.50 and for the Odeon they are £3.50, £3.00 and £2.50 on sale now.

The band will be augmented for the tour reflecting the instrumental additions on their latest album 'Remain In Light', which was released recently ago by Sire. David Byrne, Jerry Harrison, Tina Weymouth and Chris Frantz will be joined by bassist Busta Cherry Jones, Parliament/Funkadelic keyboard player Bernie Worrell, former Zappa and Bowie guitarist Adrian Belew (all of whom are featured on the album), percussionist Steve Scales and back-up girl vocalist Dollette McDonald.

The Tour

Talking Heads
New York

"WE'RE NOT like we used to be," announced David Byrne from the stage of the Central Park Festival in New York. As with many of Talking Heads' sentiments, Byrne's line had a somewhat contradictory meaning.

Yes, the band configuration for this show was a first for America, involving an impressive ten piece set-up, including two back-up singers (Nona Hendryx was one), plus old Bowie guitarist Adrian Belew and ex-Funkadelic keyboardist Bernie Worrell. Yet the band were still doing the usual manic songs about indecision and displacement — the old mental traumas re-defined in a new setting.

An outdoor arena is a difficult challenge for such a subtle anti-flash unit as Talking Heads. Even in their earliest days, six years ago, performing as a three piece in that sweaty shoe box CBGB's, they sometimes had trouble projecting the length of the place. Now with ten players in the fold, David Byrne's introverted lyrical manias were transformed into extroverted raves. Their show here in the open air proved as captivating as the band's best performances in a four piece in such small halls as the Bottom Line.

The distance the band has progressed was neatly encapsulated by the journey from the opening number (the lonely, brooding 'Psycho Killer') to the closing (a joyous, communal 'Take Me To The River'). Just the pure sight of ten musicians on stage is an immediate sign of communalism, bolstered here by the emphasis on funk-dance music, much of it from the soon-to-be-released new Talking Heads LP. Longer, more rhythmic versions of the funk songs from 'Fear Of Music' also dominated, like a churning rendition of the waltz 'Cities' and 'I Zimbra'.

It was interesting to see an audience of nearly 7,000, most of whom probably wouldn't be caught dead in the vicinity of a disco album, happily bopping to the funk rhythms of the certified-cool Heads. Also striking, in terms of past perspective, was in seeing T.H. (formerly the ultimate white bread band) really getting down. Of the newer numbers, the immediate standout was a steamy African chant which seemed to be titled 'The Heat Goes On', featuring alluring vertigo vocals — somewhere off-key, even threatening to throw off the entire rhythm. Yet it was just such a joyous twist that kept the tension going. The only problem through the show was the backup singers, who sang in clipped tones too restrained for the charging music.

One number where it all came together best was 'Life During Wartime', a song which best points out the band's command of internal irony. The song facetiously turns war into a disco just as the lyrics protest that very concept (it's a lot like the song 'Heaven' where the final resting place is interpreted to be a bar). 'Life During Wartime' is also hyper-relevant to the current air of American jingoism, giving the whole number a chilling edge.

Talking Heads have always delivered all these feelings on record, but faced with the open air (as Byrne has written: 'The air can hurt you too'), they pulled a surprising coup, filling the entire arena with their sharp wit and musical perfection complexes. They may now be yelling instead of talking, but then again, perhaps that's more the proper tone for today.

JIM FARBER

TALKING HEADS: hyper relevant

days of their careers). The chance to see them live by 1980 was unfortunately not as abundant for their UK fans.

For those who were there, the two nights in Hammersmith (the Palais on 1st December and the Odeon on 2nd) were packed. Even before the shows, there was excitement in the respective bars for what was to come.

Although the number of musicians on stage had more than doubled compared to when Talking Heads had last performed in the UK, the sound didn't come across as overdone. The rhythm section of Weymouth and Frantz was still at the vital forefront. The assistance that Harrison had on guitar and keyboards enhanced what was possible. This all gave Byrne the scope to lead as a confident frontman. The non-Talking Heads musicians added something phenomenal to the proceedings with Belew having plenty of room to play some amazing guitar solos. Overall, the nine-piece band were on top of their game, able to play well as an ensemble and yet, not without subtlety where the songs required it.

A local UK paper considered the album a necessary purchase for those unable to obtain tickets for the small offering of dates that Talking Heads had listed for the UK: "Talking Heads continue to walk successful across a very high tightrope with their latest album, *Remain In Light*. One wrong move and they could fall into self-parody. On *Remain In Light* a few hesitant steps can be seen though the Heads still maintain their balance with style, but not without the help of Brian Eno. Perhaps it's not an original thought but the best album of 1981 could be produced by the combined talents of David Bowie, Eno, Robert Fripp and Talking Heads. Currently they all move in similar directions. *Remain In Light* however, proves Talking Heads is still producing some of the best modern music to be heard. The jaunty manic rhythms are there and singer David Byrne still sounds as if he's the loneliest man in the world. And unlike the band's three previous albums you can hear most of

The Tour

TALKING HEADS IN

TALKING HEADS are to play two London dates at the beginning of December, their first since January this year. The concerts will be at London Hammersmith Palais on December 1, where all tickets cost £3.50, and London Hammersmith Odeon 2, £3.50, £3.00 and £2.50. When asked if Talking Heads would extend their appearances to the rest of the UK, a spokesman for the band said that while the London dates were the only ones to be confirmed, there was a possibility that more might be added.

what he's singing. The influences Byrne and Eno picked up on their recent African trip are also evident, softening the sharper sounds on the previous albums. There's also less of Byrne's brittle rhythm guitar. If you are one of those unfortunate enough not to have tickets for the band's two Hammersmith concerts next month, *Remain In Light* is a must. In fact, it's a must anyway." (Interestingly, at the time, another local UK paper referred to Byrne as "America's Bowie".)

Towards the end of the Remain In Light tour was the performance at the Palazzo dello Sport in Rome on 17th December 1980. Whilst many dates of the tour are sadly nothing but a memory for those who were there, this one was captured on film, intended for TV broadcast. Although it was never officially released, the footage has been circulated abundantly and is easy to get hold of. A strong performance was documented that night and serves as testament to the fact that Talking Heads were at their peak during not only this gig, but the period overall. It is a document of talented individuals making an incredibly good sound together, all whilst having the confidence to perform pieces of strong rhythmic complexity.

The concerts that took place in Dortmund, Germany on 19th and 20th December 1980 played host to not only Mike Oldfield, but also Dire Straits and Roxy Music. Talking Heads' performance that took place on the 20th was broadcast, in part, on Germany's *Rockpop* show on 27th December and on the UK's *The Old Grey Whistle Test* on 31st January 1981.

The final date of the tour — 28th February 1981 — was in Tokyo at the Nihon Seinenkan. Two shows were played there. One started at 5:30pm and the final one started at 9:30pm. The audio of the latter was recorded unofficially and distributed as a bootleg by the name of *Tokyo Final Night*.

Overall, this era of Talking Heads' career incorporated an iconic aspect of performance style. *Melody Maker* considered in August 1981; "Byrne's live performances with Talking

The Tour

Heads have found him becoming increasingly absorbed with dance and physical involvement. The tribal and ethnic strands which have become woven into *My Life In The Bush Of Ghosts* and *Remain In Light* have influenced Byrne's attitude to performance radically."

That's not to say that Byrne's energetic approach to performance was lacking previously though! *New Musical Express* considered in July 1979; "Byrne's own performance is staggering. It encapsulates everything that seemed interesting in Bowie and Ferry all those years back and creams them with a totally original approach. His thyroid glands are pumping towards the red zone, danger level." To which Byrne was quoted; "I get taken over by the live act. The adrenalin rush for me is complete. I seem to be running around while everyone else is in slow motion. It's exciting but frightening and wonderful. The only thing that disappoints me is when a crowd shouts out for the better-known songs — that's not likely to boost your opinion of an audience. But audiences will tire of the obviously manipulative stuff. My own perspective when I go to a show is I hate that pop star routine. I assume that our audience wants to be treated with respect. We made it a rule never to use artificial crowd responses. Then again, we try and play in decent places — comfortable halls or clubs with good acoustics. Of course, we don't always succeed. Sometimes the venues are far from ideal. The bouncers manhandle the audience when there will only be a few troublemakers on Quaaludes. Promoters tend to assume the worst. Because of a minority they mistreat the majority. I admit that a lot of times we end up playing in terrible places, but you just try your best."

Talking Heads - *Remain In Light*: In-depth

Chapter Four

Legacy

Both *Melody Maker* and *Sounds* named *Remain In Light* the best album of 1980. The *New York Times* included it in its unnumbered shortlist of top ten records released that year. *New Musical Express* ranked it as the sixth best record of the year and *The Village Voice* ranked it at number three.

Even after the immediacy of its release, *Remain In Light* continued to make an impact. It was certified gold by the Canadian Recording Industry Association in February 1981 after shipping 50,000 copies. The Recording Industry Association of America gave it the gold status in September 1985 after shipping 500,000 copies.

In 1989, *Rolling Stone* listed *Remain In Light* as the fourth best album of the decade. In 1993, *New Musical Express* placed it at number eleven in their Fifty Greatest Albums Of The '80s list (and at number sixty-eight in their Greatest Albums Of All Time list).

In 1997, *The Guardian* — having collated a range of opinions from renowned critics, artists, and radio DJs, — placed the album at number forty-three in their list of the 100 Best Albums Ever. In 2003, VH1 listed it at number eighty-eight as part of their 100 Greatest Albums countdown. Notably, the longevity of the interest in *Remain In Light* has far succeeded the musical era in which it was made and released.

Ever the thoughtful artist, what would Eno have done differently given the chance to have another crack at *Remain In Light*? He told *Melody Maker* in February 1981; "With *Remain*

Talking Heads - *Remain In Light*: In-depth

In Light, I think at the moment that the experiments that particularly interested me worked, but I feel we didn't take them far enough. For instance, the idea of the layered vocals. I wish I had gone a lot further with that. It is an idea I've been fascinated by for some years, and will explore further in the future, but we only really grasped the idea near the end of recording, and as the songs on that album developed very late in the recording process, there wasn't the time to extend the layered vocals idea as far as I wanted. One of the other main things we started developing that pleased me was the interlocking instruments idea — instead of having a few instruments playing complex pieces, you get lots of instruments all playing very simple parts that mesh together to create a complex track. For example, there were five or six basses on 'Born Under Punches', each doing simple bits that tie together. There's one track on that album, 'Listening Wind', that has a lovely feeling and is closest to my current mood — it has a mysterious, dark, slightly lost quality, and there is some of that feeling on *Bush Of Ghosts*. The most obviously different idea about that album is the use of found voices, although I don't feel it to be unique anymore."

Such was the abundance of African influences in Byrne and Eno's music that in some interviews with the press, they embraced the opportunity to address questions surrounding whether they had essentially taken their own bastardised understanding of the music and manipulated it for their own gain without any true, authentic experience of it. In every instance, when Byrne and Eno discussed this aspect of their music, they did so with diplomacy and intelligence.

Given Byrne's continuing absorption with African and tribal musics, regarding charges of "musical imperialism" levelled against him, he told *Melody Maker* in August 1981; "Ah, right, that's come up a few times. Brian and I were talking about it the other day because it's come up so often. I think there's a tendency on the part of the critics to see using other people's cultures — or aspects of something in another culture — by Americans as imperialism. But when musicians in another part of the world do it, it tends to be embraced with open arms. There's no question that something like reggae started off with a lot of borrowed things from rhythm and blues and lots of other sources. There's some music in Africa that's a real mishmash of influences."

Eno told *New Musical Express* in July 1980; "Yesterday I decided not to talk about Africa. My thoughts on it are only from a perspective of my mind as I haven't been in black Africa at all. I've been thinking about it so much and my thoughts are unclear. So perhaps I should stick with something I'm more able to discuss. But I hope to be there in two or three months, I hope to live there for a while... Psychedelia has always appealed to me. I never lost the sense that it was an interesting style to use. The difference is in the amount of prominence one gives it. You can either feature it or you can use it within a context, so it's like it has a sort of geographical function. Right now I have a whole psychedelic African vision... discovering this whole *continent* of people who have a different and optimistic outlook — and who look as though they're not making such a big mess — that's really given me a different feeling. I think whatever answers we're going to find in the next few years, a lot of them will come from Africa. Just as the east was a very important influence for the last fifty years or so, I think Africa will become that important an influence. God, I can't wait."

Explaining how he got interested in Africa, Eno expanded; "The truth is that it was two things — African music and black women I met. Seeing people who never have any doubts that their being was completely linked from the head to the toes and that there wasn't any separation, and that sexuality was a thing of the mind and body, not just the body and not just the mind. And that the universe was a place charged with erotic possibilities — that's really the sense I get and it seems the sense they have. Also, the sense of sexuality being something sublime, inseparable from every other social function. For instance, you see girls involved in the high life dances in Nigeria and they're doing incredibly sexy dances, but what the records are singing about are ethical and religious problems and they're very serious records. But there isn't a dichotomy there. People don't think 'Why's she dancing like that when there's this music on?'. It doesn't work like that, there is a continuity there which I find very attractive. And which I probably won't measure up to, I'm sure. I'm not of that frame of mind, I'm just an admirer of it at the moment. Maybe it's something which will develop."

Regarding the African influence, Byrne told *New Musical Express* in December 1981; "Recently I have been working somewhat along those lines, but nowhere near as much as the musics from those cultures do. I'm still stuck with the four, five-minute song — I still find that a comfort, I still find that a comfortable thing to work with. Whereas people in those cultures will go on playing for hours at a stretch, the same groove, on, but lots of variety and breaks in it; it'll involve from one thing to another and go through a series of movements but it's essentially the same piece that lasts for *hours*. And I'm not used to that. I grew up with a three-minute song. I've worked my way up to six minutes or seven minutes, but that's about as far as I've got so far. But I suppose in the context of a pop song it is fairly different than a rock or a standard pop song."

He told *New Musical Express* in November 1980; "For something to have the effect that it's supposed to have, it's not necessary to understand all of it. I read in a book on voodoo that the structure of the rituals, the drumming, the singing, the chanting, the symbolism of the rituals isn't understood by half of the people that are participating. It isn't necessary for them to understand. I'm inclined myself to think about it, to try and understand it, but that's not necessary. And what's even more

Legacy

amazing I think is that it's not even necessary to *believe* in it. For instance, if I were to get involved with one of those things, I wouldn't have to believe in Jesus or whatever, I would probably just get carried away along with the rest of the people, which is really a testament to the power of those things. The feeling one gets from it isn't cathartic or purging, it's not that you let off steam or whatever, it's more like a mystical communion. And it's not some sort of psychological thing, it's more social in a way. The nature of that kind of music implies different parts and different rhythms, that all *mesh*. Not some sort of personal explosion, which tends to be what a lot of rock music is about."

New Musical Express considered; "David Byrne, being somewhat impressionable, became absorbed in Brian Eno's discovery of Africa. The two of them set off like explorers into the California desert to try to capture the feeling of the bush in the sagebrush. They failed and had to resort to recording *My Life In The Bush Of Ghosts* in a more prosaic setting, using "found vocals" from the radio as their bush of ghosts. I don't want to suggest that Byrne is a vacillating lump of jelly without a mind of his own, but it's obvious that even more impressionable Brian Eno made the running here. Byrne's interest in musical anthropology surfaced in a short piece he wrote for *High Times* soon after *Buildings And Food*, and several songs on *Fear Of Music*; most notably 'I Zimbra' bore an ethnic trace that pointed to the hypnotic swirl of words and rhythms that characterises *Remain In Light*. However, Eno, being the more systematic of the two, probably helped put the idea into practice."

Byrne's article in *High Times* was a clear indication of the thought he'd put into exploring a range of influences, conveying information such as "There is a Chinese legend that the emperor Huang-ti "ordered" the invention of music in 2697 B.C." and "The Pima Indians of the American Southwest believe that songs already exist and that the composer's job is to "untangle" them."

Talking Heads - *Remain In Light*: In-depth

The creative approach to making *Remain In Light* marked a development in Byrne's songwriting. In response to the question of "Do you write dispassionately — selecting words, sentences, scraps — or do you get lost in language?" Byrne told *New Musical Express* in December 1981; "I'm impassioned about it — but at the same time I have to organise it, because undirected passion has no affect at all, it's just someone yelling into the wind. Unless it's organised it's really ineffectual. So I have to take passionate outbursts or words and phrases that I think will be highly charged or I can sing in a highly emotional way and organise them, be dispassionate when I organise the song... I've been trying to get a wider range of emotions in the stuff I've been doing and in Talking Heads' material, and I think I've succeeded a little bit — not always as much as I'd like to but a little bit. I've just gone back and listened to a lot of our older stuff recently, since we've been mixing some old live tapes as well as newer ones, and I can really hear that I really did sound like someone — a really berserk person! And now I think at times I would go a little bit too far the other way, try to sound a little bit too dispassionate or too controlled. So I guess I should try to strike some sort of balance between the two."

Byrne had always had an interesting approach to lyrics. Of how he handled them in the earlier days of Talking Heads, he told *New Musical Express* in December 1979; "My sole consideration overall — the main thing which I could look back and say yes, this is true about these numbers — is the fact that in terms of the lyrics, I wanted to strip everything down to the level of it being nothing more than what one hears in a conversation. I felt lyrics were becoming long-winded and pointless, that they needed to be far more to the point. It wasn't so much a case of what was being said, so much as the way it was being put across. I couldn't stand all the unnecessary embellishments, the idea of lyrics as poetry that demanded reams and reams of verses, most of them superfluous or just pointless... Most of the time I see lyrics more as exercises in relating differing points of view, more than anything else. Like you can take virtually any one of those songs in which I'm playing a character who's narrating a certain viewpoint and you can be sure to find another song of mine which has someone taking exactly the opposite stand. There's the guy in 'Don't Worry About The Government' who's a really satisfied suburban homebody type and then there's the guy on the plane in 'The Big Country' who has nothing but disgust for that lifestyle... In 'Psycho Killer' the guy singing it is flipping out from an internal crack-up. He's hysterical, but his hysteria is all to do with this fuse that's blown in his brain. The guy I depict in 'Life During Wartime' is a very rational type."

Weymouth told *New Musical Express* in November 1980; "David does not come to the band with a full-blown song. He comes with a riff maybe, if that, maybe nothing. The whole band puts it together and then David writes really terrific words. I really love his writing. He's so good at it and it's something he won't give up as long as he's singing the songs because he feels he can sing them with more conviction if he knows what they mean."

For Byrne and Eno the success of *Remain In Light* was such that it was always going to be a tough album to follow. (The term "follow" is being used loosely here: the pair had recorded *My Life In The Bush Of Ghosts* prior to working on *Remain In Light*. Some of the former needed to be re-recorded after the latter though, as previously indicated, due to a legal dispute regarding the use of the "found" voices.)

The *Los Angeles Times* said in March 1981; "Talking Heads' *Remain In Light* was one of the most venturous new wave experiments of 1980 — a fusion of American funk forms and African rhythm modes that seemed as rousing and instinctive as Michael Jackson's *Off The Wall*, yet as methodical and modern as Steve Reich's cyclic sonatas. Now with *My Life In The Bush*

Talking Heads - *Remain In Light*: In-depth

Of Ghosts, Talking Heads' leader David Byrne and producer Brian Eno take their avant-funk obsessions one step further into an area that might roughly be called ethno-abstractionism. In place of the impelling crossweaves of melody and rhythm that permeated *Remain In Light*, Byrne and Eno have fashioned kinetic collages out of disconnected guitar, percussion and synthesiser fragments, and have even fabricated vocal parts from snippets of songs, sermons and dialogue lifted from radio and other sources... Granted, *My Life In The Bush Of Ghosts* is mesmeric and commendable, but only rarely does it manage to overcome its own self-pleasing air of conceptualism and take the leap of faith into communion and carnality that made *Remain In Light* such provocative and unfettered fun. The difference between the two records comes down to something like the difference between idea and epiphany — and in the end, that's some difference."

In the same month, another journalist writing for *LA Weekly* considered; "Nothing can be more misconceived than the notion that Brian Eno and David Byrne's *My Life In The Bush Of Ghosts* is about Africa. Whatever its apparent influences or cursory designs, this album, in its danger and fatalism, hair-trigger desperation and over-the-top faith, is about nothing if it's not about America — the way, coincidently enough, rock and roll is about America, the way blues is about America co-opting African rhythms, slapping them in chains and bartering them for profit. To say that Eno and Byrne's new music is African is to presume that Africa is the antithesis of America, that they exist in alien contention, both geographically and in the psyche. But of course, Africans were forming a lot of the basic American axioms from the first; and here is music to take us back, somewhere through the last unopened plantation-cellar door, to make the connections that have been short-circuiting the white man's consciousness all along."

"*My Life In The Bush Of Ghosts* exists, of course, in

Legacy

tandem with Talking Heads' *Remain In Light* of last year, in which punk was gang-raped by funk to spawn a disturbed and dazzling progeny. But even though *Bush Of Ghosts* was recorded before *Remain In Light*, ostensibly as something of a warm-up, it is in fact just the opposite: a culmination so reckless and consuming that the Talking Heads edition sounds like a retreat in comparison. In all likelihood, *Remain In Light* was, more or less, just that — the popularisation, even the intended conventionalisation, of *Bush Of Ghosts*' strategies, though such an idea would have astounded most of us six months ago, upon hearing the earlier record. Personally, I was never really sold on *Remain In Light*. Important and admirable though it obviously was, its most profound concerns always seemed cerebral; if I didn't know better, I would have thought it was an experiment by former art school students or something. Eno, who produced *Remain In Light*, has made his reputation in the past as an avant-gardist dabbling in ambience scores and furniture music, welding them from time to time with pop ideas. Byrne, Talking Heads' writer and singer, has always had pop ideas of his own, but they've not often sounded deeply-felt; rather, they come across like meticulously developed quirks, contrived and sometimes laboured to death in the band's musical think-tank."

"The irony is that Eno, the avant-gardist, has often made music genuinely brighter, warmer and more emotionally evocative than popsters Talking Heads; and I have no doubt that the lack of gut-level conviction in much of *Remain In Light* is Byrne's responsibility: by the time the theories of *Bush Of Ghosts* were applied to the Talking Heads record they had been baked too long, considered too deliberately and predicted too precisely. In contrast, *My Life In The Bush Of Ghosts* is filled with discoveries that probably surprised even its authors; and in fact the new album most recalls not *Remain In Light*, but Eno's and Byrne's respective masterpieces, *Another Green World* (1975) and *Fear Of Music* (1979), in terms of its open-ended shimmer in the first case and hell-bent-for-paranoia tension in the second."

After five years of writing, recording and touring the world, Talking Heads were burnt out. They'd released four albums and needed some time off. It was after the Remain In Light tour that the members of the band went off to work on different projects independently (as did the additional musicians). *Melody Maker* reported in August 1981; "Other members for the latest nine-piece Talking Heads line-up have also been busy — guitarist Adrian Belew has been conspiring with Robert Fripp and drummer Bill Bruford, while bassman Busta "Cherry" Jones has been recording and also stood in on bass with Gang Of Four after bassist Dave Allen departed. Meanwhile, David Byrne has been finding still more new bearings. He's been occupied with writing a soundtrack for a ballet by the Twyla Tharp dance company, who recently visited London for some performances at the Sadler's Wells Theatre."

In 1981 Byrne released an album called *The Catherine Wheel*. It was the music on this that was used for a dance production by Twyla Tharp. Harrison managed to secure a record deal to do an album of his own material. Husband and wife team Frantz and Weymouth joined forces to put together a side project called Tom Tom Club. Their eponymous debut album spawned the hits 'Wordy Rappinghood' and 'Genius Of Love'.

Weymouth said in later years; "Tom Tom Club was a breath of fresh air musically and for us personally. We injected the dance element from Talking Heads and lightened it up."

And of course, having the scope to work on new projects outside of Talking Heads meant that each member could explore new ideas and methods of working. Having just released his first solo album, *The Red And The Black*, Harrison said in 1981, "I suppose there's always that element, when you work with other people, where you'd like to see something else being done. There's always compromise, which is one of the great things about groups. But occasionally you'd like to try to see something all the way through. For me, I had always arranged or helped co-write songs, but had never forced myself to be the sort of person who had to do everything. I think it was something I had to prove to myself... If we had done those songs with Talking Heads, I probably wouldn't have been the singer, so probably that was one of the best things — to put myself in the position where I had to do it."

Time away from each other made the members of Talking Heads appreciate what they were able to do together as a group and in 1983, they released the album *Speaking In Tongues*.

Notably, even prior to recording *Remain In Light*, it's plausible that Talking Heads felt they needed some time off. *New Musical Express* considered in July 1979; "Talking Heads are in an intriguing position. Their creative and practical muse is at a peak, but the demands on their attention span are getting too big. Both Byrne and Frantz, the original members, claim to have reached the watershed as far as touring goes. For the drummer this means a tolerance of the rock lifestyle which he began by despising." To which Harrison was quoted; "We were always anti-stardom. Where the Stones were sexy we were frigid, where Elton John was glamorous we'd be ordinary. Now I feel more sympathetic to those people. We didn't try to be intellectual or smartass, but because of our college backgrounds people assumed we were cerebral. I find a fair amount of passion in the music — it isn't a mental exercise." As was Byrne; "I'd like to be doing other things. Touring puts you in a rut. It takes up most of the year, and the way it's organised you waste so much time. That bothers me more than anything else. You're there to play, but it only takes an hour to do that."

As long as the break between *Remain In Light* and *Speaking In Tongues* was, it may have been the case that a new project could have emerged sooner after Talking Heads' 1980 album:

a case of schedules not quite syncing perhaps? Byrne told *New Musical Express* in December 1981; "I had a talk with Chris and Tina a couple of weeks ago... We were talking about going back to a more traditional song form, working within that idiom and yet still using all the things we've learned... I don't know how it'll work out. We haven't started rehearsing yet."

Overall, the working rapport — or sometimes lack thereof — between the members of Talking Heads has always been an interesting one. *New Musical Express* commented in December 1979; "I recall the only previous time I'd encountered Byrne in an interview situation, when the three other members of the band were present and Byrne was painfully uncomfortable — a state of affairs made all the more excruciating at times when he'd attempt an explanation of sorts regarding some detail in one of his songs, only to be greeted by somewhat derisive chuckles from other members. Tina Weymouth would virtually scold him like a mentally defective son for his inability to articulate logically for the band. Group interviews are now virtually a thing of the past, I was told by one who should know. A similar source had also hinted that Talking Heads were due to take a lengthy sabbatical, commencing very, very soon. No permanent break-up, mark you. Just an extended holiday for a band who've been relentlessly working ever since the deal with Sire was signed."

New Musical Express reported in November 1980; "I was taken aback to hear Byrne blithely admit that he hadn't talked about his feelings towards their new music with the rest of the group. Maybe he's just like that, and their internal balance is stronger than it seems, but someone who saw the new band on stage in Los Angeles was moved to remark that it looked as though Byrne had got himself a new band and had forgotten to get rid of the old one, a suggestion which all four of them shrug off."

Of course, the release of *Remain In Light* marked the end

Legacy

of Talking Heads' collaboration with Eno. Weymouth told *New Musical Express* in November 1980; "Eno taught us to relax in the studio, which I think was his intention all along. He found that we were very willing to be experimental, as he was, and he was delighted with that — to find a band that would allow him to race everybody's track and not get artistically sensitive and precious about it. And I think we've done it now. I told him that I always envisioned doing a trilogy with him, and once we'd done this studio album, that would be the end of our collaboration. He said I think that's quite right, and probably we won't be working with him again."

In 2018, Beninese singer Angélique Kidjo released a song-for-song cover of *Remain In Light*. Her approach to the album was produced by Jeff Bhasker. Describing herself as a fan of 'Once In A Lifetime', her intention was to pay tribute to the album by placing emphasis on the African music influence.

Remain In Light could not possibly exist if it were not for the African influence. Could such an album be achieved again by a commercially successful group today? It's hard to say, but if it happened, it would certainly be a standout end-product (assuming that it wouldn't be an outright copy of what Talking Heads tried — and succeeded — to do).

Perhaps it's important not to overstate the extent to which the African influence was at play on *Remain In Light* though. In later years, Byrne has said that, ultimately, there was "less Africanism in *Remain In Light* than we implied... but the African ideas were far more important to get across than specific rhythms." And: "Even though the music didn't always sound particularly African, it shared that ecstatic communal feeling." He referred to the album's final mix as a "spiritual" piece of work, "joyous and ecstatic and yet it's serious".

'Once In A Lifetime' has gone on to be a significant pop culture reference over the years since its release. In 1996, Kermit the Frog performed a version of it for an episode of

Muppets Tonight. In it, Kermit was suited in the same style of big suit that Byrne wore for the original video. The Rock And Roll Hall Of Fame lists 'Once In A Lifetime' as one of the 500 songs that shaped rock and roll. In 2021, *Rolling Stone* named it the 81st best music video.

And of course, whilst 'Once In A Lifetime' is easily the song that most people probably remember from Talking Heads' 1980 output, what the band achieved overall during that period of their tenure went far beyond that. Not only is *Remain In Light* a stand-out album but also, what was achieved in terms of performing it live was arguably a milestone not only for Talking Heads, but in terms of what can be achieved when utilising an expanded ensemble of musicians to replicate the complexities of what was achieved in the studio — all at a time when the technology for looping and sequencing was so primitive that the reliance was on the musicians themselves to play an idea on repeat.

In 2017, the Library of Congress declared *Remain In Light* as "culturally, historically, or artistically significant" and elected to preserve it on the National Recording Registry. Understandably, based on the musical innovation and what is to simply be enjoyed about the album, many consider it to be Talking Heads' magnum opus.

Discography

Personnel

Talking Heads
David Byrne – lead vocals, guitar, bass guitar, keyboards, percussion, vocal arrangements
Jerry Harrison – guitars, keyboards, percussion, backing vocals
Tina Weymouth – bass guitar, keyboards, percussion, backing vocals
Chris Frantz – drums, percussion, keyboards, backing vocals

Additional Musicians
Brian Eno – keyboards, percussion, guitar, bass guitar, backing vocals, vocal arrangements
Nona Hendryx – backing vocals
Adrian Belew – guitar, Roland guitar synthesiser
Robert Palmer – percussion
José Rossy – percussion
Jon Hassell – trumpets, horns

Production
Brian Eno – producer, mixing
Dave Jerden – engineer, mixing
John Potoker – additional engineering, mixing
Rhett Davies – additional engineering
Jack Nuber – additional engineering
Steven Stanley – additional engineering
Kendall Stubbs – additional engineering
David Byrne – mixing
Greg Calbi – mastering

Design
Tina Weymouth – cover art
Chris Frantz – cover art
Walter Bender – cover art assistant
Scott Fisher – cover art assistant
Tibor Kalman – artwork
Carol Bokuniewicz – artwork
MIT Architecture Machine Group – computer rendering

Track Listing

All lyrics by David Byrne, except for 'Born Under Punches (The Heat Goes On)' and 'Crosseyed And Painless', which were written by David Byrne and Brian Eno. All music composed by Byrne, Eno, Chris Frantz, Jerry Harrison and Tina Weymouth.

Side One
1. Born Under Punches (The Heat Goes On) (5:49)
2. Crosseyed And Painless (4:48)
3. The Great Curve (6:28)

Side Two
1. Once In A Lifetime (4:23)
2. Houses In Motion (4:33)
3. Seen And Not Seen (3:25)
4. Listening Wind (4:43)
5. The Overload (6:25)

Expanded CD reissue unfinished outtakes
9. Fela's Riff (5:19)
10. Unison (4:50)
11. Double Groove (4:28)
12. Right Start (4:07)

Talking Heads - *Remain In Light*: In-depth

Original US releases, October 1980:
Sire SRK 6095, LP
Sire M8S 6095, 8-track
Sire M5S6095, cassette

US Reissues:
Sire 6095-2, CD, 1984
Sire, R2 76452, Hybrid DualDisc, 2006
Sire, R1 70802, LP, 2006
Sire RCV1 70802, LP, 2018

Original UK releases, October 1980:
Sire SRK6095, LP
SRKC 6095, cassette

UK Reissues:
Sire SIR K 56 867, LP, 1984
Sire 7599-26095-2, CD, 1997
Sire 8122708021, LP, 2013
Sire RCV1 70802, LP (red vinyl), 2018

Singles:

Born Under Punches (The Heat Goes On) / Cities (Live version)
Sire 7PP-23, Japan, 1980

Crosseyed And Painless / The Great Curve
Sire 600 363, Germany, 1980

Once In A Lifetime / Seen And Not Seen
Sire SIR 4048 January 1981, UK
Sire SRE 49649, February 1981, USA

Houses In Motion (Special Re-Mixed Version) / Air
Sire SIR 4050, May 1981, UK

Houses In Motion / The Overload
Sire SRE49734, May 1981, USA

Talking Heads - *Remain In Light*: In-depth

Tour Dates

Please be aware that the following list may not be exhaustive. It is derived from corroboration of information from posters, ticket stubs and reviews.

1980

August 20th	Hampton Beach Club Casino, NH, USA (cancelled)
August 23rd	Heatwave Festival, Bowmanville, ON, Canada
August 27th	Wollman Rink, Central Park, NY, USA
October 17th	Greek Theatre, Los Angeles, CA, USA
October 18th	Greek Theatre, Los Angeles, CA, USA
October 19th	Arlington Theatre, Santa Barbara, CA, USA
October 20th	Palladium, Hollywood, CA, USA
October 22nd	Zellerbach Hall, Berkeley, CA, USA
October 23rd	Warfield Theatre, San Francisco, CA, USA
October 24th	Warfield Theatre, San Francisco, CA, USA
October 26th	Aragon Ballroom, Chicago, IL, USA
October 27th	Oriental Theatre, Milwaukee, WI, USA
October 28th	Northrop Auditorium, University of Minneapolis, MN, USA
October 30th	Masonic Auditorium, Detroit, MI, USA
October 31st	John Carroll University Gym, University Heights, OH, USA
November 2nd	Radio City Music Hall, NY, USA
November 3rd	Radio City Music Hall, NY, USA
November 4th	Capitol Theatre, Passaic, NJ, USA
November 5th	Stage West, West Hartford, CT, USA
November 6th	University of Hartford Gymnasium, Bloomfield, CT, USA

Talking Heads - *Remain In Light*: In-depth

November 7th	Ocean State Theatre, Providence, RI, USA
November 8th	Emerald City, Cherry Hill, NJ, USA
November 9th	Emerald City, Cherry Hill, NJ, USA
November 11th	Warner Theatre, Washington, DC, USA
November 12th	Palace Theatre, Albany, NY, USA
November 14th	Orpheum Theatre, Boston, MA, USA
November 15th	Orpheum Theatre, Boston, MA, USA
November 17th	Agora Ballroom, Atlanta, GA, USA
November 18th	Agora Ballroom, Atlanta, GA, USA
November 20th	Agora Ballroom, Dallas, TX, USA
November 21st	Armadillo World Headquarters, Austin, TX, USA
November 22nd	Agora Ballroom, Houston, TX, USA
December 1st	Hammersmith Palais, London, UK
December 2nd	Hammersmith Odeon, London, UK
December 3rd	Theatre Mogador, Paris, France
December 4th	Pavilion Baltard, Nouget Sur Marne, France
December 6th	Theatre Mogador, Paris, France
December 8th	Theatre de Verdure, Nice, France
December 9th	Palais D'Hiver, Lyon, France
December 10th	Forest National, Brussels, Belgium
December 11th	Jaap Eden Hall, Amsterdam, Netherlands
December 14th	Metropol, Berlin, Germany
December 15th	Palalido, Milan, Italy
December 16th	Palasport, Bologna, Italy
December 17th	Palasport, Rome, Italy
December 19th	Westfalenhalle, Dortmund, Germany
December 20th	Westfalenhalle, Dortmund, Germany
December ?	?, Munich, Germany

1981

February ?	?, Kyoto, Japan
February 23rd	Festival Hall, Osaka, Japan
February 24th	Aichi Public Welfare Annuity Hall, Nagoya, Japan
February 26th	Shibuya Public Hall, Tokyo, Japan
February 27th	Sun Plaza Main Hall, Tokyo, Japan
February 28th	Nihon Seinenkan, Tokyo, Japan (two shows – 5:30pm and then 9:30pm)

Talking Heads - *Remain In Light*: In-depth

HEADS HEAD FOR UK

TALKING HEADS are coming to Britain in early December to play their first concerts here with their new and enlarged band, which caused a sensation at its debut in the Toronto Heatwave festival two months ago.

Their visit is restricted to just two shows in London — at the Hammersmith Palais (December 1) and Hammersmith Odeon (2). Promoters Straight Music have still to confirm the support act, but it's expected to be U2. Tickets are on sale now at the box-office and usual agents priced £3.50 only (Palais); and £3.50, £3 and £2.50 (Odeon).

The four-piece nucleus of the Heads remains as David Byrne (vocals and guitar), Tina Weymouth (bass), Jerry Harrison (keyboards and guitar) and Chris Frantz (drums). But they are now supplemented by bassist Busta Cherry Jones, Parliament/Funkadelic keyboardist Bernie Worrell, guitarist Adrian Belew, percussionist Steve Scales and back-up girl vocalist Dollette McDonald. The result, according to *NME's* Richard Grabel in his Heatwave review, is startlingly different from anything they've previously attempted.

The Heads' new album 'Remain In Light', produced by Brian Eno, is released by Sire this week — and they'll be featuring material from the LP in their new stage act.

David Byrne sports influential new haircut. Pic: Joe Stevens

Page 12 SOUNDS September 6, 1980

Pic by Hugh Brown

RECEDING HAIRLINES HAVING FUN: *To satisfy the almost insatiable appetites of all you hordes of* **Eno** *and* **Dave Byrne** *fanatics out there crushed by the news that the toupeless twins' elpee is 'on ice', here's some hot tips about the lad's exploits in the hotbed studio situation.*

Entitled 'My Life In The Bush Of Ghosts', bits were recorded in LA and bobs in San Francisco utilizing Bri's nouveau working strategy of 'if it (music) makes you frown it's not worth doing.'

They also seem to have employed a rather unique set of music making objects to boot. Bri and Dave played ukelele, amplified guitar case and floor, coiled spring over car muffler, guitar, piano, bass and assorted unidentifiable South American instruments (of torture?) Also roped in were **Mingo Lewis** *and* **Prairie Prince** *of* **Tubes** *fame on percussion and drums, apparently forced into using rickety drum kits and plastic waste buckets in the name of Art. Chart certs on vinyl include a manic track featuring a politician's voice from a radio phone-in show who'd been indiscreet with a young boy in public and was on the air apologising. The vocals thus go 'um uh um uh um uh' interspersed with 'he made a mistake, he made a mistake'. Another zippy number shows the duo's funky roots and makes a major lift of a* **Sly Stone** *bassline. The whole caboodle should surprise everyone who thought they had Eno and Byrne pegged. Here come the* **Funkadelic Heads.**

Talking Heads - *Remain In Light*: In-depth

In-depth Series

The In-depth series was launched in March 2021 with four titles. Each book takes an in-depth look at an album; the history behind it; the story about its creation; the songs, as well as detailed discographies listing release variations around the world. The series will tackle albums that are considered to be classics amongst the fan bases, as well as some albums deemed to be "difficult" or controversial; shining new light on them, following reappraisal by the authors.

Titles to date:

Jethro Tull - Thick As A Brick	978-1-912782-57-4
Tears For Fears - The Hurting	978-1-912782-58-1
Kate Bush - The Kick Inside	978-1-912782-59-8
Deep Purple - Stormbringer	978-1-912782-60-4
Emerson Lake & Palmer - Pictures At An Exhibition	978-1-912782-67-3
Korn - Follow The Leader	978-1-912782-68-0
Elvis Costello - This Year's Model	978-1-912782-69-7
Kate Bush - The Dreaming	978-1-912782-70-3
Jethro Tull - Minstrel In The Gallery	978-1-912782-81-9
Deep Purple - Fireball	978-1-912782-82-6
Deep Purple - Slaves And Masters	978-1-912782-83-3
Rainbow - Straight Between The Eyes	978-1-912782-96-3
Jethro Tull - Heavy Horses	978-1-912782-97-0
Talking Heads - Remain In Light	978-1-915246-01-1
The Stranglers - La Folie	978-1-915246-02-8
David Bowie - The Rise And Fall Of Ziggy Stardust And The Spiders From Mars	978-1-912782-92-5